WINNING THE MONEY GAME MADE EASY

Building assets and wealth for your future

WINNING THE MONEY GAME MADE EASY

Building assets and wealth for your future

By Bradley L. Gummow

Four Seasons Publishers
Titusville, FL

WINNING THE MONEY GAME MADE EASY
Building assets and wealth for your future

Mr. Gummow is an investment officer of a major New York
Stock Exchange member firm and is a Registered Investment
Advisor Affiliate of said firm. Said firm has no interest or
liability in Winning The Money Game.

For information contact: Four Seasons Publishers
P.O.Box 51, Titusville, FL 32781

PRINTING HISTORY
First Printing 1999

ISBN 1-891929-14-3

PRINTED IN THE UNITED STATES OF AMERICA
1 2 3 4 5 6 7 8 9 10

To my family for your love, devotion, encouragement, and support.

To my now-deceased grandfather for having instilled a good work ethic.

To my clients and friends who have made this journey rewarding.

Success is not a destination, but rather, a journey.

Mr. Gummow may be contacted directly at

4343 E. State Street
Rockford, IL 61108
(815) 229-2699

TABLE OF CONTENTS

Chapter 1

Establishing Your Investment Objectives

"If you don't know where you're going, how do you expect to get there?"

Basil S. Walsh

The Importance of Planning

Why have a plan at all? If you have a particular goal or destination in mind, following a plan is the quickest, most efficient way to reach it. Builders have blueprints; teachers have lesson plans; coaches have game plans. The random approach has its merits if you like surprises, but I'll venture to guess that you have something more specific in mind regarding your future financial security.

Let's illustrate this point with a simple exercise that will take just a few minutes. Look at Figure #1 on page 3. Next, get a watch or clock with a second hand to time yourself. Locate the number "1" in the upper right hand corner and circle it. Now your task is to find as many numbers as you can, in sequential order, within sixty seconds. Get ready; get set; go!

If you were able to get to number "9", you did very well indeed.

Look at Figure #2 on page 4. You will notice at a glance that it looks a lot like Figure #1. With the exception of the lines dividing the numbers into quadrants, it is identical to Figure #1. You are going to repeat the sixty-second drill; this time, however, I'll give you a clue. Starting with the number "1" in the upper right hand corner and move counter clockwise. You will find number "2" in the upper left corner, number "3" in the lower left, and number "4" in the lower right. Return to the upper right for number "5", to the upper left for number "6", and so on. Ready? Go!

I'll bet you found at least twice as many numbers this time. What was the difference? You had a plan, of course!

Figure 1

First Number Exercise

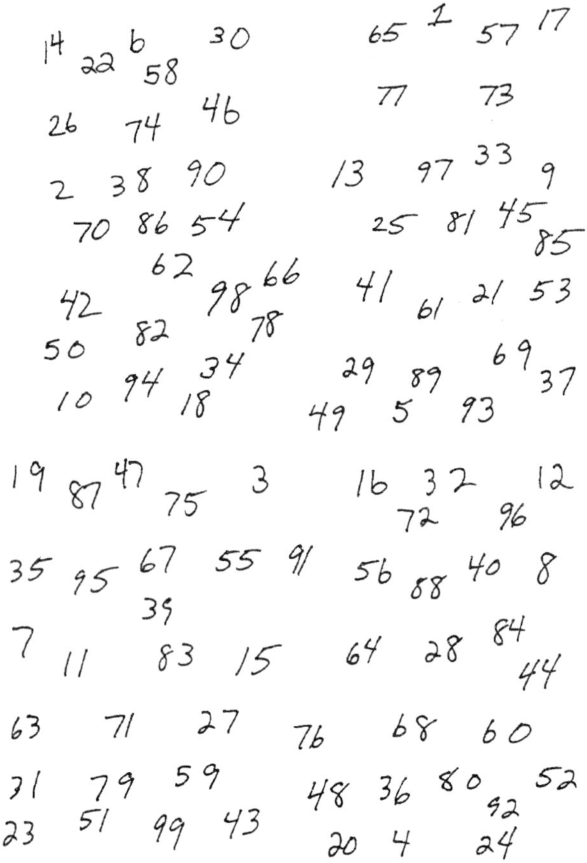

14 22 6 58 30   65 1 57 17

26 74 46   77   73

2 38 90   13 97 33 9

70 86 54   25 81 45 85

62 98 66   41 61 21 53

42 82 78

50

10 94 34 18   29 89 69 37

49 5 93

19 87 47 75 3   16 32 12

72 96

35 95 67 55 91   56 88 40 8

39

7 11 83 15   64 28 84 44

63 71 27 76   68 60

31 79 59   48 36 80 52 92

23 51 99 43   20 4 24

Figure 2

Second Number Exercise

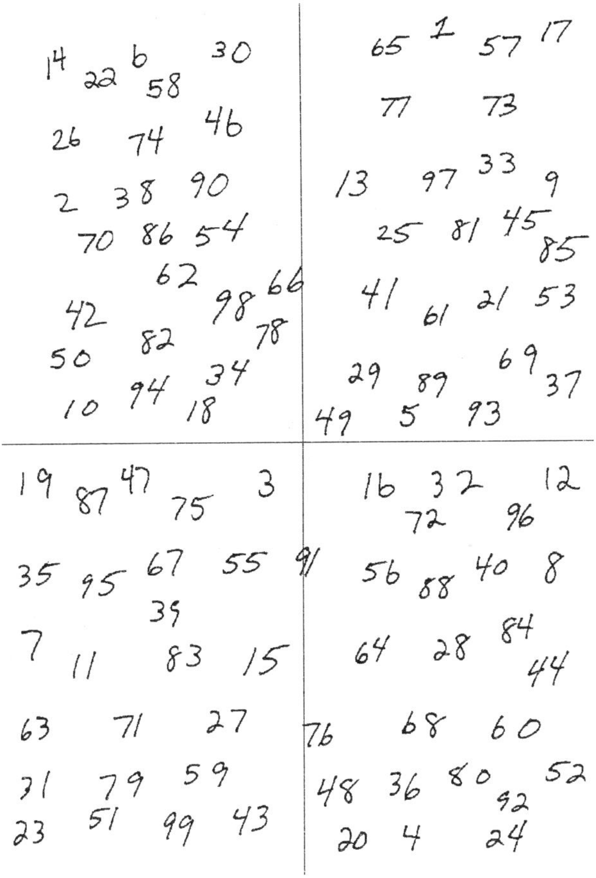

You probably have some concept of what you'd like your life to be after you leave behind the "daily grind" for good, but that does not necessarily constitute the type of systematic plan that will get you there. Chances are, you plan to be without a job at some point in your life, but you will certainly not be able to survive without an income. Will Social Security, your 401k plan, and a savings account provide you with the purchasing power you need to sustain the lifestyle you desire? Probably not. Will a patchwork of investments — a hot stock here, a few CD's there, and so on — pick up the slack? Not necessarily. A well-executed investment plan, however, directs the money you are earning to become another "wage earner" contributing to your retirement and future financial needs.

In the course of this book, I will walk you through a systematic, step-by-step approach to building a secure financial future through effective planning and management of investments. If you follow the six steps in order, you will learn to direct, rather than imagine your long- and short-term financial future. You will be better equipped to develop and manage your Personal Investment Plan suited to your specific needs and desires. While it may not be as simplistic as locating numbers in sequential order, it will become simpler when you begin to recognize that there are discoverable patterns in the investment process. You will also discover that establishing an integrated pattern in your investments will increase the earning power of your money.

Getting Started

A Personal Investment Plan is a concrete reality, not an abstract concept. Consider yourself its architect and builder. Before you can begin the process of building your

Personal Investment Plan, you must gather all the necessary materials.

You will need to get together all of your financially related documents. These may include statements of checking and savings accounts, NOW accounts, Money Market Funds, certificates of deposit, brokerage firm statements, IRA accounts, job-related retirement accounts — any record of where your money is and what it is doing for you there. You may need to request information from each appropriate agency if you do not have a readily available statement of one or more of your accounts. For example, your personnel department at work will provide you with pension information. Upon written request (See Sample Worksheet #1 on the next page), the Social Security Administration will provide you with a free statement outlining your earning history, your total-to-date paid in Social Security taxes and an estimate of your future benefits. It is vital to the success of your plan to have accurate and comprehensive records of your finances.

Once you have gathered all of your financial documents, they may appear to have as much connection to each other as the numbers scattered about the page in Figure #1.

Since it is part of the information gathering process, please fill out Worksheet #1, "Request for Earnings and Benefit Estimate Statement" now, and send it to the Social Security Administration.

You will fill out the other worksheets in turn, when the pertinent information is discussed. As you do this, you will begin to see an order and relationship (or lack of an order and relationship) among them that will enable you to start to evaluate whether your investments are best serving your interests. As we progress further, you will develop a clearer picture of evaluation criteria which will help you see when and how to consider alternatives and make adjustments.

What you do with your options is your decision. Providing you with a context within which to make informed decisions is my goal in the six-step process.

Grab your calculator, and let's begin.

SOCIAL SECURITY ADMINISTRATION

Albuquerque Data Center
P.O. Box 4429
Albuquerque, New Mexico 87196

SOCIAL SECURITY...It never stops working!

SOCIAL SECURITY ADMINISTRATION

Request for Earnings and Benefit Estimate Statement

Social Security is a program that touches the lives of nearly all Americans. Although many people think of it as only a retirement program, it is actually a package of protection that provides for you and your family when you retire, become severely disabled, or die. Social Security is a base you can build on, now and in the future, with savings, other insurance, and investments.

To help you plan for your own financial future, I am pleased to offer you a free statement which shows your Social Security earnings history, tells you how much you have paid in Social Security taxes, estimates your future Social Security benefits, and provides some general information about how the program works.

To receive your statement, please fill out the form on the reverse, and mail it to us. You should receive your statement in 6 weeks or less.

DORCAS R. HARDY
Commissioner of Social Security

Request for Earnings and Benefit Estimate Statement

To receive a free statement of your earnings covered by Social Security and your estimated future benefits, all you need to do is fill out this form. Please print or type your answers. When you have completed the form, fold it and mail it to us.

1. Name shown on your Social Security card:

_____

First   Middle Initial   Last

2. Your Social Security number as shown on your card:

☐ ☐ ☐ – ☐ ☐ – ☐ ☐ ☐

3. Your date of birth: _____ _____ _____

Month   Day   Year

4. Other Social Security numbers you may have used:

☐ ☐ ☐ – ☐ ☐ – ☐ ☐ ☐

☐ ☐ ☐ – ☐ ☐ – ☐ ☐ ☐

5. Your Sex: ☐ Male   ☐ Female

6. Other names you have used (including a maiden name):

_____

_____

7. Show your actual earnings for last year and your esti mated earnings for this year. Include only wages and/or net self-employment income subject to Social Security tax.

   A. Last year's actual earnings:

   $ ☐ ☐ ☐ , ☐ ☐ ☐ . ☐0☐ ☐0☐

   Dollars only

   B. This year's estimated earnings:

   $ ☐ ☐ ☐ , ☐ ☐ ☐ . ☐0☐ ☐0☐

8. Show the age at which you plan to retire: _____

9

9. Below, show the amount which you think best represents your future average yearly earnings between now and when you plan to retire. The amount should be a yearly average, not your total future lifetime earnings. Only show earnings subject to Social Security tax.

Most people should enter the sam eamount as this year's estimated earnings (the amount shown in 7B). The reason for this is that we will show your retirement benefit estimate in today's dollars, but adjusted to account for average wage growth in the national economy.

However, if you expect to earn significantly more or less in the future than what you currently earn because of promotions, a job change, part-time work, or an absence from the work force, enter the amount in today's dollars that will most closely reflect your future average yearly earnings. Do not add in cost-of-living, performance, or scheduled pay increases or bonuses.

Your future average yearly earnings:

$ ☐ ☐ ☐ , ☐ ☐ ☐ . 0 0

10. Address where you want us to send the statement:

I am asking for information about my own Social Security record or the record of a person I am authorized to represent. I understand that if I deliberately request information under false pretenses I may be guilty of a federal crime and could be fined and/or imprisoned. I authorize you to send the statement of my earnings and benefit estimates to me or my representative through a contractor.

_____

Please sign your name (Do not print)

_____   _____
Date   (Area Code) Daytime Telephone No.

ABOUT THE PRIVACY ACT
Social Security is allowed to collect the facts on this form under Section 205 of the Social Security Act. We need them to quickly identify your record and prepare the earnings statement you asked us for. Giving us these facts is voluntary. However, without them we may not beable to give you an earnings and benefit estimate statement. Neither the Social Security Administration nor its contractor will use the information for any other purpose.

10

Establishing Your Investment Objectives

Now that you understand the importance of having a plan to accomplish your financial goals and have gathered the materials with which to build it, let's begin to assemble it.

The logical first step in achieving your goals is to understand what they are and when you expect to reach them. Step One, then, is to list your objectives, begin to list the financial goals (and obligations) that you project. Notice how your financial future has been conveniently divided into three parts beginning with the short-term and ending with the long-term.

As your teacher, I feel obligated to tell you that there is no right or wrong answer here; this is not a test, and if you forget something you will come back and add it without penalty! In fact, the entire six-step process is cyclical in nature. You will be repeating it regularly — each time more efficiently and with more insight.

What are your financial responsibilities in the future? Consider them all. Do you plan to fund college educations for your children? Do you have a plan to buy a new home or a vacation home? At what age do you plan to retire? What hobbies and enrichments do you plan to pursue? Travel? Your own education? Will you be caring for a parent, child, or other dependent?

Now that you have listed your goals for the future, you will need to take stock of the present to see if you are heading in the right direction. Step Two, then, is to take inventory of your current investment portfolio so that you will be able to determine if your combination of investments will fund the future you envision.

How much do you currently spend just "surviving" in the current economy? How much can you afford to invest for your future? What will a college education cost at the time you need to finance it? What will your housing costs be? How will the rate of inflation affect your

your purchasing power?

Unless your list is full of moral, intellectual, or spiritual growth projections, each of your objectives has a specific price tag. To establish a more concrete picture of the cost of your future and the power of your income to purchase it, you will examine the information you provide on Worksheets #3-#6 and the data provided in Figures #3-#7.

It is now time to take inventory! Yes, the task gets a bit tedious at this point. It only hurts for a little while, however, and must be performed before you can continue. Fill out the following worksheets:

  #3 Financial Planning Worksheet
  #4 Education Planning Questionnaire
  #5 Retirement Questionnaire
  #6 Asset Allocation Survey

Please be honest in filling out these forms. Remember: no pain, no gain.

Bradley Gummow

Worksheet #2
Objectives/Liabilities Planning Sheet

```
    25      35      45     55      65       75
20      30      40     50      60      70       80
                      AGE
```

List Objectives

Short-Term (0-12 months)   _____

_____

_____

Intermediate-Term (1-10 yrs) _____

_____

_____

Long-Term (10+yrs)   _____

_____

_____

Financial Planning Worksheet

Name	Occupation	Age

Spouse's Name	Occupation	Age

Address

Phone (Home)	Phone (Business)

Your Social Security No.	Spouse's SSN

Children	Age	Dependent	Self-Supporting

What are your major concerns when managing your financial affairs? Indicate the order of importance by number (i.e. "1" = most important

☐ Building Wealth

☐ Increasing current income

☐ Security for my family

☐ Reducing my tax liability

☐ Providing for retirement

☐ Planning for future needs (e.g. education, leisure activities)

☐ Hedging against inflation

☐ Providing liquidity for sudden cash needs

☐ An easier way to manage my finances

14

Bradley Gummow

What are your current investment objectives? Indicate the order of importance by number (i.e. "1" = most important).

☐ Long-term growth - Safety very important

☐ Long-term growth - Will accept some risk to meet investment objective

☐ Speculative - A greater degree of risk may be tolerated

☐ Income with safety

☐ Income with some risk

☐ Taxes are a concern - Need tax reduction/deferral/ exemption

☐ Liquidity - including CD's, Money-Market Funds

Household Income	Your Income	Spouse's	How much tax did you pay last year?
Employment Investment, etc.	————	————	
Non-recurring (bonus, sale of asset, etc.)	————	————	$ _____
Will income vary greatly?	☐yes ☐no	☐yes ☐no	

Which sources do you use for personal financial planning? Indicate the order of importance by number (i.e. "1" = most important).

☐ Insurance Agent   ☐ Lawyer   ☐ Investment Advisor   ☐ Bank

☐ Accountant   ☐ Broker   ☐ Financial Planner   ☐ Myself

Have you had a written financial plan prepared?   ☐ yes   ☐ no
If so, when? ————————————————
By whom? ————————————————

15

Winning The Money Game Made Easy

Estate Plans	Yes	No	**Has your will been reviewed in recent years?**		
Do you have a will?	☐	☐			
				Yes	No
Does your spouse have a will?	☐	☐	Yours	☐	☐
Have you created a trust(s)?	☐	☐	Spouse's	☐	☐
Are you beneficiary of a trust(s)?	☐	☐	When _____		

Type of Retirement Plan	**Yours**	**Spouse's**
Company Pension or profit sharing	☐	☐
Government/non-profit or teachers	☐	☐
Individual Retirement Account (IRA)	☐	☐
Keogh Plan/401k/403B	☐	☐

Has your life insurance been reviewed within the past three years?   ☐ Yes   ☐ No

	Your Insurance	Spouse's Insurance
Number of policies	_____	_____
Total face amount	$ _____	$ _____
Total annual premiums	$ _____	$ _____
Total cash value	$ _____	$ _____
Loans outstanding	$ _____	$ _____

Are you currently able to combine savings, checking, investments, and credit card purchases in a single account?
☐ Yes   ☐ No

What is the current market value of your home?
$_____

What is the amount of the outstanding mortgage, if any?
$_____

Do you own:	Yes	No
House	☐	☐
Condominium	☐	☐
Cooperative	☐	☐
Second house	☐	☐

Estimate your current net worth:

☐ Under $100,000   ☐ $100,000 - 250,000

☐ $250,000 - 500,000   ☐ $500,000 - 750,000

☐ $750,000 - 3,000,000   ☐ Over $3,000,000

Assets

Do you own...	Yes	No
CD's		
Stocks		
Control or Restricted Securities		
Options		
Commodities		
Precious Metals/Coins		
Real Estate Holdings (other than your own home)		
Government Bonds		
Gov't Nat'l Mortgage Assn.		
Corporate Bonds		
Preferred Stocks		
Municipal Bonds		
Unit Investment Trusts		
Money-Market Funds		
Mutual Funds		
Tax-Deferred Annuities		
Tax Shelters		
Real Estate		
Limited Partnerships		
Whole Life Insurance		
Term Insurance		
Disability & Health Insurance		

17

Do you have a brokerage account at another firm?
☐ Yes ☐ No
If you wish, name of firm:

Please list below any additional assets

SAVINGS

Money-Market Funds	CD's	Rate	Maturing
	$	%	
	$	%	

Savings Accounts (include Credit Unions)

$

Other (identify)

$

INVESTMENTS (Attach additional pages, if necessary)

Stocks	Approx. Purch. Date	Approx. Purch. Price	Quantity

18

Bradley Gummow

Bonds/Unit Investment Trusts	Approx. Purch. Date	Approx. Purch. Price	Quantity

Real Estate Interests and Limited Partnerships	Approx. Purch. Date	Approx. Value

Shelters	Approx. Purch. Date	Approx. Value

19

Winning The Money Game Made Easy

Retirement Plan Assets	Approximate Value

What do you expect from your Financial Consultant?

_____

_____

Regarding other Brokerage Accounts

Are you dissatisfied with :　☐ Service　☐ Communications

☐ Performance　☐ Other _____

List any other family or related account(s) *(please attach copy of recent statement)*

Account Name:	Account Number	At another firm?

Remarks - Notes - Additional information that would assist in this review

_____

_____

_____

_____

20

Bradley Gummow

Worksheet #4
Education Planning Questionnaire

Name _____

Social Security No. _____

Account No. _____

Name of Child _____ Age _____

Home State _____

Age to Start College _____

Name of University/College Location _____

_____

Commuter or Campus Resident _____
In-State or Out-of-State _____
Any Additional/Other Expenses_____

Amount (if any) of Current Education Fund

_____

After-Tax Yields you Expect to Receive on your
Education Fund _____

Worksheet #5
Retirement Questionnaire

Part 1 - General Information

Name: _____
Address: _____
Phone: Home: _____ Work: _____
Date of Birth: _____ Current Age: _____
Spouse D.O.B. _____ Current Age: _____

Part 2 - Retirement Planning Information

1) What do you expect the average rate of inflation to be over the next 10 years? _____ %

2) At what age do you anticipate taking retirement income? _____

3) Estimate of monthly retirement living expenses in today's dollars? (refer to Part 6) $ _____

4)At what age do you anticipate receiving social security benefits? _____
   What percent of social security benefits do you qualify for (100%, 75%, etc.): _____ %
AND/OR
   If you know the exact dollar amount: $_____

5) At what age does your spouse anticipate receiving social security benefits?_____
   What percent of social security benefits does your spouse qualify for:_____
AND/OR
   If you know the exact dollar amount:$_____

6) Do you anticipate any extraordinary income?____
If so, the amount $_____
and year/years that it would occur _____

7) Do you anticipate any extraordinary expense?____
If so, the amount $_____
and year/years that it would occur _____

Part 3 - Present Company Retirement Plan

1) Can you receive an annuity payment from your
pension plan?   Yes   No
   If so, what would the approximate monthly
   payment be? $_____

AND/OR

2) Can you receive a lump sum distribution from your
pension plan?   Yes   No
   If so, what is the current value: $ _____
   and return _____ %

AND/OR

Approximate value at retirement: $_____

Part 4 - Present Capital Available

	Account Values	Rate of Return
Taxable (Savings, MM, CD's)	$	%
Tax Deferred (Annuity/Insurance)	$	%
Tax Free (Muni/ Mutual Fund)	$	%
Equities (Stocks/ Mutual Fund)	$	
Other (Partnership, % etc.)	$	%
Retirement Accounts (IRA, 401k)	$	%

Monthly Additions to Retirement Capital_____

Additions - 1 = level, 2 = increasing
        (please circle one)

Winning The Money Game Made Easy

Part 5 - Tax and Current Income Data

1) Filing Status (1=Single, 2=Joint) _____

2) Taxable income prior to retirement: $ _____

3) Taxable income during retirement: $ _____

4) Tax bracket before retirement: _____ %

5) Tax bracket after retirement: _____ %

Part 6 - Current Budget Information, Monthly Living Expenses

Item	Today	In Retirement
Mortgage/Rent		
Property Taxes		
Insurance		
Gas,Oil, Electric, Water, Phone, etc.		
Other		
Total Housing Expenses		
Savings/Investment		
Food (including dining out)		
Clothing/Personal Care		
Transportation		
Medical Care		
Education		
Entertainment/ Vacations		
Charitable Contributions		
Other		
Total Monthly Expenses		
Total Annual Expenses (multiply by 12)		

Bradley Gummow

ASSET SURVEY
(Asset Allocation Worksheets)
Prepared for:

Name _____ Age _____

Spouse's Name _____ Age _____

Address_____

City_____ State ____Zip _____

Home Phone _____ Work Phone _____

Will?☐ Yes ☐No Living Revocable Trust?☐ Yes ☐No

Risk Level: ☐ Moderately Conservative ☐ Agressive

Life Insurance Death Benefit_____

Residence_____

Earned Income	
Social Security Taxable	
Social Security Non-Taxable	
Pensions	
Retirement Distributions	
Other	
Annual Expenses	
Annual State & Federal Taxes	

Client Objectives:

1) _____

2) _____

3) _____

4) _____

5) _____

Stocks

Individual stock or stock mutual funds, also preferred stocks:

Assets	Amount	Income

Property Ownership

Rental properties and net rental income, limited partnerships:

Assets	Amount	Income

Tangible Assets

Includes Assets such as gold/silver coins, natural resource funds:

Assets	Amount	Income

CURRENT ASSET ALLOCATION

Cash/Cash Equivalents
All assets that are liquid or mature in less than 1 year:

Assets	Amount	Income or %	Tax-able	Non Tax-able

Fixed Income
Interest-generating assets that have maturities of greater than one year:

Assets	Amount	Income or %	Tax-able	Non Tax-able

Winning The Money Game Made Easy

At this point, we will examine some of the financial conditions that will impact your projected income and expense figures for your future. This discussion will provide you with insight that will help you to evaluate your personal situation.

Tax Planning, for 1998 and Beyond

In his campaign, Bill Clinton said that he planned to raise taxes — on the rich. True to his word, that's exactly what he did.

It is absolutely essential that you understand the impact of new and existing taxes on your income and on your investments.

Since we are at the "taking inventory" step in our process, you will need to assess your current tax situation before our tax strategy can be developed. Figure #3 (on page 29) provides tax law highlights for the year 1998. Figure #4 (30) shows the 1998 tax rates. Where do you fit in?

Using your most recent tax returns and Figure #4 to help you estimate your 1999 amounts, calculate your marginal tax bracket and your projected 1999 tax.

Your 1998 tax determinations will signal your course for 1999. If you expect to be in the same or lower tax bracket in the future, consider the merits of deferring income and accelerating deductions. If you expect to be in a higher tax bracket, consider accelerating income and deferring deductions. If you anticipate that the capital gains tax rates will drop in the future, consider deferring capital gains.

In summary, do not select a unilateral course based on a cursory or superficial examination. Consider both specific instance and its integration into the broader, longer range tax profile.

Finally, don't forget to consult your tax advisor before making any contemplated changes.

Figure #3
Recent Tax Highlights

Individual Tax Rates
The top marginal tax bracket of 39.6% begins at the
following levels:
Single individual	$278,450
Joint return	$278,450

Capital gains rate
The top rate is set at 20% on long-term capital gains,

Individual alternative minimum tax
The rate is 26% on incomes to $175,000; 28% over
$175,000 under review. (Always consult tax counsel on
tax related matters.)

Phase-out of personal exemptions
The deduction is phased out gradually for single tax
payers and joint filers with incomes exceeding
$124,500.
(This, too, will be adjusted, in my opinion.)

Social Security
Employers and employees are subject to different tax
rates at different wage base levels. Beginning in 1994,
the Medicare portion of Social Security is 1.45% of all
income.

Base levels are now up for review. Self-employed taxpayers pay approximately twice as much tax as individ-

uals. However, self-employed taxpayers may deduct one-half of their Social Security tax liability for regular tax purposes, under current law.

The maximum deductible payment to a 401(k) plan increases each year. Contribute as much as you can to defer taxes and build wealth. Maximum is currently $10,000 for 1998.

Figure #4
1998 Federal Tax Rates

Tax Rate	Single	Married/Joint Return
15%	$0-$25,350	$0-$42,350
28%	$25,350-$61,400	$42,350-$102,300
31%	$61,400-$128,100	$102,301-$155,950
36%	$128,100-$278,450	$155,950-$278,450
39.6%	$278,450+	$278,450+

Note: Long-term capital gains realized from the sale of assets are taxed at a maximum rate of 20% 1998, and are currently under review in Congress.

Tax-brackets are subject to change at the whim of those in Washington, D.C.

Always, always consult tax counsel.

As a pure, capitalistic, money-grubbing Republican, I can't help but add the following: The new tax law is aggressive in that it punishes those that create success for themselves. Here's a great example: The new 10% surtax, (which virtually adds a whole new marginal bracket), all filers, (single or joint), will pay an additional 10% on taxes on income over $278,450 in taxable income. This kills incentive — when will Washington learn?

Here's another: The Medicare payroll tax now applies to all salary income.

And another: Itemized deductions and personal exemptions for high-income taxpayers will have their limits extended.

Somebody tell Washington that the so-called rich employ the so-called middle class. I submit that Washington should encourage the rich to take risks, (build more, buy more, etc.), to create new jobs. End of lecture.

Education Funding: A Learning Experience

For many parents today, providing a college education for their children is more than just a dream; it is a necessity. Due to factors such as constant, rapid technological advances and increased competition for career opportunities, the work force of tomorrow needs the advantage a college education can provide. Unfortunately, the cost of this education may be prohibitive to many who have set their sights on a future that requires it.

The assessment of your ability to foot the bill for a college education depends upon an understanding of what that education will cost at the specific time you will be shopping for it. When you take inventory of your current savings or investments, you need to consider a number of factors relative to the cost of a higher education. These factors will direct your strategy in planning to meet your child's future education needs.

Over the past several years, the price tag for education has been rising at a faster rate than inflation. If you wait until the last minute to fund your child's education, the actual cost may come as quite a shock. Whether your child is five months or five years old, the time to start investing in her education is now.

How much will you need to save? That is the 100,000-dollar question! Almost literally, as a matter of fact. Based on an inflation fate of 7% (a rate slightly below the average for most schools), one year of education costing approximately $9,200 today, would cost over $25,000 in fifteen years. Given that inflation will not stay on hold while your child finishes the remaining three years, his total education bill might easily exceed that $100,000.

The College Board of Education has estimated that the cost of a four-year, public university education will be $88,000 by the year 2008. Costs will, of course, vary with specific school choices. The College Entrance Examination Board provides data, updated annually, on tuition costs for over 3,000 colleges, universities, community colleges and technical schools throughout the United States. They also provide estimates of expenses for room and board, books, personal items and other applicable costs. (Your investment firm should be able to provide an education Funding Analysis at no cost to you.)

Figure #5 (33) shows a sample cost analysis for the University of Illinois-Urbana for the year 1996 and alternatives for achieving the income needed to fund a four-year program there. Identifying the costs and time frame in which to meet them are the first steps in putting together the education funding plan. They form part of the decision-making basis for choosing among investment alternatives.

Bradley Gummow

Children's Education Needs
BRADLEY F. GUMMOW EDUCATION FUND
July 1, 1993

GOAL:

To provide $9,190 per year for each child (1993 dollars). Assuming 7.00% inflation, the projected total education costs are $49,984. Your present fund of $7,300 is not adequate. If the fund earns 8.00% annually, then you should deposit an additional $4,972 in 1993.

Alternatively, an additional $27,954 invested today at 8.00% would pay the projected education costs.

SUMMARY FOR EACH CHILD

Child	Needs Added Annual Savings of	For	Which Pays Education Costs for	Starting In Year
1) Bradley	4,972	7 yrs	4 yrs	1996

ANNUAL BREAKDOWN OF EDUCATION FUND

Year	Paid to School	PAID by Mr. E: To School	To Fund	Paid from Fund	Ending Balance
1993	0	0	4,972	0	13,254
1994	0	0	4,972	0	19,684
1995	0	0	4,972	0	26,628
1996	11,258	0	4,972	11,258	21,970
1997	12,046	0	4,972	12,046	16,087
1998	12,889	0	4,972	12,889	8,823
1999	13,792	0	4,972	13,792	0
Total	49,985	0	34,801	49,985	

Winning The Money Game Made Easy

College COST Explorer (TM) 1992
  Copyright (c) 1991 by College Entrance Examination
  Board

U ILLINOIS URBANA
URBANA, IL 61801

Forms required: FAF and FFS
Closing Date: none
Priority Date: 3/15   Home State: IL

BUDGET:	<-->RESIDENT
92-93 Tuition & Fees:	$ 3,140
Add'l out-of-state:	$ N/A
Books & Supplies:	$ 420
Room & Board:	$ 4,040
Transportation:	$ 380
Personal Expenses:	$ 1,210
Other:	$ 0
Total Budget:	$ 9,190
Estimated EFC:	$ -------
Estimated Need:	$ -------

FINANCIAL AID PROFILE

% freshman receiving aid:	80%
number applied for aid:	3800
number judged to have need:	3200
number w/need offered aid:	3100
number offered full amount:	-

DISTRIBUTION OF AID

% in grants/scholarships:	54%
% in loans:	32%
% in jobs:	14%

34

TUITION AND/OR FEE WAIVERS FOR

Adults:	No
Children of alumni:	No
Senior citizens:	Yes
Minorities:	No
Family members enrolled:	No
Employee's family:	Yes
Unemployed (or children (of unemployed):	No

SPECIAL PAYMENT PLANS

Credit Card:	No
Installment:	Yes
Prepayment discount:	No
Deferred payment:	No

GRANTS/SCHOLARSHIPS
College has need based aid: Yes

	need based+	non-need based
Academics:	Yes	Yes
Music/Drama:	No	Yes
Art:	No	Yes
Athletics:	No	Yes
Job skills:	No	No
State/Dist. residence:	Yes	Yes
Leadership:	No	Yes
Alumni affiliation:	No	No
Religious affiliation:	No	No
Minority affiliation:	Yes	Yes

It is certainly true that the younger your child, the longer you have to accumulate funds for his education. Starting early and saving in an investment vehicle that provides a rate of return over and above the rate of inflation will help you secure an appropriate education for your child. In any case, even if your child is only a few years away from college, it is never too late to start a funding program. Duration is certainly a factor in determining the wisdom of one investment over another in a particular instance. You must tailor your choice of investments to time constraints among other things. Later on in this book, I will discuss in more detail the considerations for choosing among the investment alternatives.

Can You Afford to Retire?

You've saved twenty, thirty, even forty years for your retirement. The kids have flown the nest. The house is paid for. Your major financial obligations are behind you. Now that you are coming face to face with the reality of retirement, can you say with reasonable certainty that your retirement income will support you through the next ten to thirty years? Too many people view retirement as a time when they no longer have to worry about saving or investing for the future. They assume that their future lifestyle will be financed adequately if they channel all their assets into a "safe" investment like a Treasury Bill or Certificate of Deposit.

Nothing could be further from the truth. Treasury Bills and CD's are very safe for meeting short-term goals and liabilities. They provide a safety of principle and ease of liquidity not readily matched by other instruments. What they don't provide is a long-term hedge against our biggest enemy — inflation. (I will be more specific about this later.)

"Hold on, we have inflation under control now," you

counter. "Why should we worry about it?" The straight-forward answer is, that even at a steady 5% inflation rate, what costs you $100 today will cost nearly $250 in twenty years. The price of survival will be almost tripled. And we, as a nation, are living longer. Have we an effective plan for financing these additional years?

One of the first things to focus on after taking inventory of your retirement portfolio is duration. Again, we are not talking about a few years. This is a long time to live off of an investment portfolio that took at least that long to build. The problem is compounded by the fact that Social Security will not provide as much of our monthly needs as we had anticipated. For 1998, a married couple who were both sixty-five and had both contributed the <u>maximum</u> amount, could hope to take home $32,308 annually, or $2,684 monthly. Is this enough to keep a roof over your head, food in your belly, and fulfill your needs and desires beyond your physical sustenance?

Figure #6 (38) provides projections for the annual savings required to achieve a desired income level at retirement, based on a retirement age of sixty-five. Does the inventory of your own retirement investments demonstrate that they will meet your needs? Chances are, you will need a more efficient plan.

Winning The Money Game Made Easy

Figure #6
Annual Savings for Retirement Income

Present Age Annual Income Goal	30	35	40	45
	Annual Savings Required			
$20,000	$1,022	$1,552	$2,409	$3,849
$30,000	$1,534	$2,332	$3,614	$5,773
$40,000	$2,044	$3,109	$4,818	$7,697
$60,000	$3,066	$4,665	$7,227	$11,546
$80,000	$4,088	$6,218	$9,636	$15,394

(This table assumes that the assets are used at retirement to purchase an annuity yielding 8% year until death.) Inflation adjustments are not included.

"But my needs will/should be relatively modest in retirement," you say. What if I told you that you needed two million dollars to retire? It's shocking, but may be true! If you're planning to retire in twenty-five years, and your 1998 household income was $100,000, you might need more than $2,000,000 of your own money — in addition to Social Security or your company pension — to maintain your standard of living. That is a conservative estimate for enough money to last for twenty years. What if you live longer? For a thirty-year retirement, you would need nearly $3,000,000! Figure #7 (see page) provides a breakdown of investment requirements for maintaining your financial lifestyle during retirement.

Even though you quit working, the job of earning an income must still be done. A substantial income prior to retirement does not protect you from downward mobility after retiring. In fact, it makes you more vulnerable. The portion of earnings replaced by Social Security to your company pension diminishes rapidly as you climb the income scale. Consequently, the more you earn, the more you'll need to depend on your investments in retirement. (Remember, the maximum annual income a couple retiring in 1998 can expect to receive from Social Security is approximately $32,208. This is assuming that the couple were both making the maximum Social Security contribution since 1951, and each retired at age 65.)

According to 1997 statistics, only 27% of your retirement income will be derived from Social Security. Company pensions will account for another 25%; IRA/Keogh, personal saving/investments and other sources will account for 15%, 12%, and 21%, respectively.

Millions of retired Americans will need to rely on resources outside of Social Security for maintaining their desired lifestyles. With careful planning and monitoring, your investments will become "breadwinners" to help make up for the shortfall left by Social Security.

Too many people rely solely on short-term vehicles such as T-Bills and Money Markets to fund their ten- and twenty-year needs, forsaking the growth opportunities equities can provides to keep ahead of inflation. Are equities volatile? Yes, as a short-term investment. No, as a long-term goals/liabilities will broaden. You will gain the insight to help you consider a range of alternatives you may previously have ignored or been aware of.

Figure #8 provides information on average annual rates of return for investments over several decades. You can see, at a glance, how a variety of investments performed over the last seven decades. The '90's look to be greater.

Figure #8

Average Annual Rates of Return
1926-1989 in percent

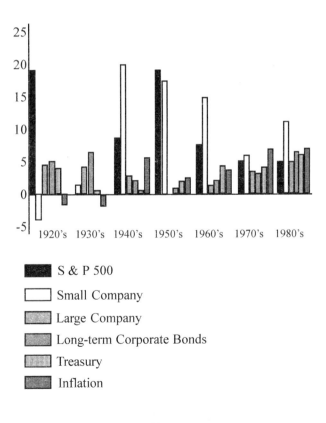

S & P 500

Small Company

Large Company

Long-term Corporate Bonds

Treasury

Inflation

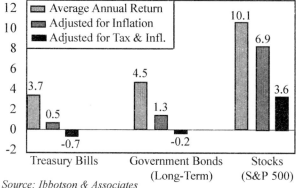

1926 - 1990 in percent

Source: *Ibbotson & Associates*

To keep pace with inflation during the years since 1970, an investor would have had to have an 8% annual, compounded growth of his income — after taxes, of course! The inflation rate today may be less, but the principle remains the same. Your money must earn better than 8% per year, on average, to beat inflation, pay taxes, and enjoy some real dollar growth. I trust that this drives home, once again, the importance of an effective Personal Investment Plan.

The Biggest Mistakes People Make With Money

A Baptist church in Atlanta had the following words on its marquee," Getting rich is no longer a sin. It's a miracle!"

I'm going to wrap up this chapter with a list of twelve of the biggest mistakes people make with money. I will not provide you with any get-rich miracles. I will, however, help you avoid some of the pitfalls of poor investment practice. These mistakes are the reasons so many folks are not enjoying the maximum earning power of their dollars. How we use money is more important than

than how we make it.

1. **They never decide what they want to accomplish with their money.** Nothing happens until someone sets a specific financial objective and then directs his or her thinking and actions toward the realization of that objective.

2. **They have no specific plan for accomplishing their financial objectives.** Most people spend more time planning their vacations than they do their entire financial future. No one would think of building a house without a set of blueprints. Yet many people try to reach a financial objective without an organized financial plan.

3. **They do not consider the impact of inflation in their planning.** They often plan for retirement, education of their children, and other future expenses, based on today's dollars. In other words, they often fail to consider the increase in the cost of living.

4. **They procrastinate in making financial decisions.** Procrastination can be the greatest deterrent to reaching a financial goal. Too many people are waiting until "the time is right" to start an investment program. For one reason or another, the time will never be "just right". Lots of valuable time can be lost through this deadly enemy — procrastination.

5. **They look for a guarantee of their dollars rather than the conservation of their purchasing power.** While guaranteeing a return of loaned dollars (i.e. savings accounts, CD's, T-bills, money markets, etc.) plus interest, these investments usually fail to return

to the lender the equivalent buying power of the original loaned dollars. For example, on November 1, 1951, one dollar bought 100 postcards. That same dollar, deposited in a U.S. Savings Bond at 5% interest after taxes, would have grown to five dollars by November 1, 1984. After thirty-three years, however, that five dollars would buy only thirty-eight postcards, resulting in a 38% loss of buying power. In order to have conserved the purchasing power for 100 postcards, that 1951 dollar would have had to compound at 8.1% annually. Nineteen dollars bought 100 postcards in 1994, less in 1995.

6. **They don't take advantage of the methods available to legally minimize their taxes.** Income taxes can often be minimized or deferred through the use of trusts, tax shelters, variable annuities, installment sales, pension and profit sharing plans, the Keogh plan, tax sheltered annuities, 401(k) plans and Individual Retirement Accounts (IRA's).

7. **They take unnecessary risks by being either too conservative or too speculative.** Some investors try to obtain such a high return on their money that they dramatically increase the probability of losing much of their capital. Others risk losing some of the purchasing power of their dollars through too conservative a guaranteed program. A less extreme program in either direction is far more prudent.

8. **They don't protect themselves against the loss of their earning power.** Approximately one-third of the people who are thirty-five years old today will be disabled for more than three months before reaching age sixty-five. (Half of these disabilities will be two years or more.) What makes it even more tragic is the fact that many of these men and women provide

all or most of the family income. Disability income insurance is one good way to make certain that if you are laid up, you won't be wiped out financially. This type of insurance is designed to provide most of the money you'll need to pay those bills when you are unable to work.

9. **They make investment decisions on the basis of emotion rather than logic.** The three questions you should always ask before making investment decisions are
   1. What is the potential reward?
   2. What is the risk?
   3. Is the potential reward worth the risk involved?

Most investors, however, ignore this risk/reward test. They let their emotions make the decisions for them, which, more often than not, will be wrong.

10. **They fail to diversify their assets.** Many times an investor will get all excited about one type of investment and commit all available resources to it. It is far more prudent to diversify your assets in several different types of investments.

11. **They don't allow enough time for successful results.** Too many people want it all right now. They become dissatisfied with an investment in a matter of months, rather than being patient and allowing several years for that investment to produce the results they had hoped for. There is no such thing as a good one-year investment program. Those who will need their money within a year should deposit that money in some form of guaranteed dollars.

12. **They don't seek professional advice on their over**

all financial program. Most people buy life insurance from an insurance salesperson, stocks from a stockbroker, and so on. They deposit their savings in a bank or savings and loan because of the guarantee and the high interest rates. They have no organized program with the "big picture" of how their assets work together. They fail to take into consideration all factors that should be evaluated in determining financial choices, such as number and age of children, temperament, income, present resources, and tax bracket. They fail to get advice from someone experienced in comprehensive investment planning.

If you hadn't come to this conclusion before, by now you are acutely aware that funding your retirement is decidedly more complex than going to the mailbox for your Social Security check. In Step One, you listed your objectives. In Step Two, you took inventory of your current assets. Now you will be better able to evaluate the merits of your investments in the next chapter. You will begin to refer to the frame of reference you have built as you reviewed the information presented in this chapter.

It is now time to go to the next step in our process to sort out our options for overcoming the limitations of our current plan of action.

Chapter 2

Asset Allocation Strategy

"The best way to keep money in perspective is to have some."

Louis Rukeyser

Ready...Fire...Aim!

That is how many people typically do their investing. If we get a few dollars in our hands — for example when a CD comes due — we can't wait to do something with it. In general, we tend to be a bit impetuous about getting that money invested somewhere, and often evaluate the merits of our decision after the fact — rather than the merits of our alternatives.

If you are heeding what you read, and following each step in order, you realize the importance of planning before taking action, and you are well on the way to taking deliberate aim before firing. In Step One, you set your sights on a target: your objectives. In Step Two, you gathered your ammunition by taking inventory.

In Step Three you will evaluate your current assets, explore alternatives and match your investments with your objectives. You will examine information that will sharpen your aim before you fire.

The Current Economy

In order to evaluate your specific economic situation more accurately, you need to take a look at the big picture, or the context in which your investments are made. One of the greatest dangers in managing finances is a narrow, shortsighted view. Understanding the cyclical nature of the economy and identifying the current position in that cycle will enable you to make prudent decisions.

In the 1990's, the scope of the economic picture is global, and we have nearly two industrialized centuries in which to view the cycle. Even the money that you deposit in a local bank is impacted by worldwide markets and events. The larger view reveals timely trends and an overall resilience in the economy.

47

Playwright George Bernard Shaw once wrote about a letter he received from an admiring female fan from Zurich. She wrote, "Dear Mr. Shaw, You have the greatest brain in the world and I have what most think is the most beautiful body and I'm pretty good-looking to boot, so maybe we ought to get together and produce the most perfect child." Not a bad proposal, eh?

After some consideration, Shaw replied, "Dear Lady, Thank you for the invitation, but after considerable thought," he continued, "what if she ends up with my body and your brain?"

The moral of this story is to consider all possible outcomes and consequences before taking action.

As a result of looking at the big picture, you will become aware that fear and pessimism are poor guiding lights for investment decisions. Throughout history, doomsayers of all kinds are almost as regular as the seasons. Notwithstanding frequent predictions of the end of the world, the sun rises every morning, so you still have a financial future to plan for.

Even as we face today's economic challenges, the United States of America is still the best place in the world when it comes to launching and piloting an investment plan. First, the U.S. has the most stable free market economy in the world. Next, we tend to have fewer economic swings and cycle changes, making the long-term picture more predictable. The stability of our government has a positive impact on economic markets, keep in mind that there's no place like home as a base from which to move toward a secure financial future.

Again, we are in a global economy. Europe and the rest of the world seem to be about a year and a half behind us in the economic cycle. Their higher interest rates and lower equity markets create many investment opportunities, as of this writing.

Germany will be the major economic power in Eu-

48

rope. The German Bundes Bank is the leading central reserve in the European community, and sets the tone for sound economic principle. As of January 1, 1993, all of the major economies of Europe commenced trading together as one large, free common market. At 350,000,000 people strong, it represented the single largest free common market in the world, at that time. The significance of such a cooperative market is that a company in Spain will be able to purchase equipment from a company in England without regard to tariff or trade restrictions and, possibly in the near future, without currency exchange problems. If the members of the European economy trade capital goods among themselves, they have an automatic, across-the-board price advantage of up to 6% over buying from the United States or Japan. We are a partner in the North American Free Trade Agreement, or NAFTA, with Canada and Mexico, which provides similar incentives in our neighborhood. GATT (the General Agreement of Tariffs and Trade), involving over 120 countries, will do even more.

With the U.S. dollar near a recent high against the Deutsche mark, could there be any investment advantages in European markets? Actually, yes. We can comfortably put a portion of our investment dollars in one of the largest free common markets in the world if we take into consideration the economic cycle rather than the current, limited point in time.

Emerging market interest rates are currently high. As these economies grow, many of these bonds could be very attractive. Other industrialized economies, i.e. Germany, are attractive. The reason — the German economy is at a crawl. What has their government done to ignite their economy? What did ours do? They will continue to lower rates. What is a good investment when rates are declining? Bonds. Look for a good bond market in Europe in the wake of declining interest rates over the next couple of years, in my opinion.

After bonds increase in value, what usually goes up next? Stocks. While our stock markets are near an all-time high right now, the performance of other equity markets around the world has been quite sluggish. In addition, 82% of the world's blue chip stocks (those having the equivalent of more than one billion U.S. dollars in assets and paying dividends of at least 4%) are outside of the United States.

A wise investment move — like the fashion adage — would be to "buy your straw hats in the fall," or to have a look at overseas companies. The combination of global economic sluggishness and a global disinflationary environment strongly supports the need for lower interest rates around the world, making it prudent to look at activity and availability of opportunity around the world.

Compounding and The Rule of 72

J. Paul Morgan hit the nail right on the head when he said that compounding may well be the eighth wonder of the world. Just what is so wonderful about it? Let's see it in action.

You are twenty years old. You save $1,000 a year (okay, you are an exceptionally mature twenty-year old) for ten years and stop at the age of thirty. You have put away 10,000 of your dollars. Your neighbor, a late starter, began saving at age thirty, but continued putting money away for thirty-five years, stopping at the age of sixty-five. He has socked away 35,000 of his own dollars. At age sixty-five, who has more money?

Assuming that the two of you received equal rates of return on your investments, you are ahead after putting away less than a third of what your neighbor did. That is the power of compounding!

Even given the dramatic power of compounding, I

most certainly do not recommend that you cease to invest in your future at any point in your life. Although you may have been ahead of the late-starting neighbor, there is no guarantee that you are ahead of the game. I can't emphasize enough the importance of having a comprehensive financial plan that includes a well-matched diversity of investments. I'll present a concrete example of this in the section on Modern Portfolio Theory. No matter when you start (and it's never too late), your attention to your investment portfolio must be systematic and regular if your dollars are to work most efficiently for you.

It is time to complete Worksheet #7 — The Rule of 72 to see just how long it takes to achieve certain financial goals. Simply put, **the Rule of 72 states that the rate of return on your investments divided into seventy-two equals the number of years it will take to double your money.** So, the higher the rate of your return, the quicker your money will double; twice the rate of return results in half the investment duration.

You are going to fill in figures on this worksheet from your personal financial picture that you provided on Worksheet #6 — Asset Allocation Survey. In light of education funding, retirement needs, and other foreseeable expenses of your future, is your current direction appropriate? Now that you know where you'd like to go, it's time to figure out how to get there. As we begin to look at factors impacting your financial profile, a new direction will likely be indicated.

Sample Worksheet #7
The Rule of 72

72 divided by rate of return = number of years to double your money

Examples:

72 divided by 5% = 14.4 years
72 divided by 7.2% = 10 years
72 divided by 10% = 7.2 years

Now plug your information into the formula.

My current assets (in dollar amount):

_____

How many times do I need to double my money?

_____

Do I have enough?

_____

Is my money working hard enough?

_____

Compounding at higher rates may very well be the eighth wonder of the world.

The Impact of Tax Brackets on Investment Decisions

When examining the impact of tax rates and determining tax brackets, we must avoid the tendency to think of these as static figures. They may vary on two levels.

In the 1960's and 70's, we experienced the highest marginal tax brackets in our history. At one point it was 70%; 70% of earned income can be taxed. In 1972, this become 50%. Now it can be, (as discussed in Chapter 1), 36% plus a surtax of 10% on incomes of $278,450 and more. Dare I label it a downward trend? We must re-evaluate our investments as tax brackets are redefined so that we can plan our investments to take advantage of tax rates.

Besides monitoring changes in the overall parameters of tax brackets, you must also take into account your "stair-step" movement up whatever is the existing scale. The brackets themselves may fluctuate by acts of Congress; your personal placement within them vary by virtue of fluctuations in your income.

Here's how the stair-step works (refer to Figure #4, page 30.) Using a joint return for a point of reference, for every dollar you make up through $42,350 you are taxed at the rate of 15%. That means fifteen cents of every dollar you earn will take a trip to Washington. You enter the 28% bracket for earned income between $42,350 and $120,300. For income of $102,300 to $155,950 you move to the 31% marginal tax bracket. Above $155,950 moves to the 36% bracket. In other words, not all of your earned income is taxed at the same rate. The first dollars will be taxed at the lowest rate 15%, the middle dollars at 28% and 31%, and the highest end of your income at 36%, plus the possible surtax on $278,450 and more (total 39.6%).

Earnings from your investment dollars, however, are always taxed at the highest rate. This means that interest and dividends from your investments will be taxed to the maximum extent. In light of this, it is important to carefully monitor rate changes. For example, watch for additional possible relief in capital gains exclusions but don't hold your breath.

How are your investment decisions guided by tax rates? Let's say you are offered a choice between a municipal bond yielding 6% or a corporate bond. Use this formula to determine the tax equivalent yield of a potential investment and what impact that specific investment will have on your income. Remember: A municipal bond is issued by a taxing district or agency i.e. state, county, city, school district, water district, etc... Therefore, most municipal bond interest is exempt from Federal income tax. Many states (ask your tax preparer) also exempt municipal bond interest.

Corporate bonds are issued by corporations and are subject to Federal and State income tax.

First, determine your marginal tax bracket. Let's use 28% as a starting point. Subtract 28 from 100 to get the difference of your tax bracket — in this case, 72 (not to be confused with the aforementioned rule of 72). Now divide the municipal bond rate of interest (6%) by the difference of your tax bracket. 6 divided by 72 equals .083. So you have an 8.3% tax equivalent yield on the municipal bond with a 6% interest rate.

When can less be more? For the purposes of discussion, I'll give you a raise that puts you in the 31% tax bracket. (Don't thank me yet.) Now the difference of your tax bracket is 69. Plugging the new difference into the formula with the municipal bond rate, 6 divided by 69 equals 8.69%.

Now we have the new 36% tax bracket. So let's also plug this rate into the formula with the municipal bond, as an example. The tax equivalent yield on the muni is now 9.37%. Do you see the significance of tax bracket on investment choices?

The lesson here is that you need to weigh more than interest rates in making your decision. If you are in the 28% bracket or above and shopping for fixed income investments, do not automatically ignore municipal bonds for corporate bonds or CD's on the basis of apparent interest yielded. Base your decision on the big picture, which includes tax equivalent yield.

Investment Categories and Modern Portfolio Theory

According to Charles Ellis, investment sage of the 1960's and 70's, "Investment policy wisely formulated by realistic and well-informed investors with long-term perspectives and clearly defined objectives is the foundation upon which portfolios should be constructed and managed over time in market cycles." These words of financial wisdom are as true today as they were when he spoke them. The 1990's standard in investment theory reflects these principles.

A recent Nobel Memorial Prize for Economic Sciences was awarded to Harry Marcowitz and William Sharp who developed the concept of Modern Portfolio Theory. According to this theory, we must balance our investments among three categories to achieve financial goals while minimizing expenses and risks over a period of time. The three categories are debt, equities, and cash.

Their study submits that a return on investments is predominately driven by asset allocation, and only secondarily by individual assets. The pie graph in Figure #10 illustrates what the study of thousands of investment portfolios revealed to Marcowitz and Sharp. Unless you are consistently — perhaps psychically — able to choose the next Apple Computer, Compaq Computer, or Walmart, the bulk of your returns will be from the proper combination of investments. They found that 93.6% of investment returns were the result of a proper balance among investment categories. Only 4.2% resulted from specific choices of investments. In other words, if you are a mere mortal like most of us, your primary focus in building an investment plan will be on the balance among types of investments, rather than on any particular stock or bond.

Figure #10
Determinant of Portfolio Performance
Modern Portfolio Theory

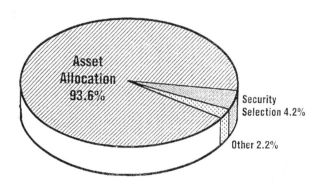

Asset Allocation is the key to financial success. Portfolio Performance depends more on assets selected than individual securities within the market.

Financial Analysis Journal. July/August 1986

I will present here a brief overview of the three investment categories. In subsequent chapters I will discuss particular types of investment opportunities in greater detail.

The **cash/cash equivalent** category represents assets that can be converted to cash in one year or less. The following are among the assets in this classification: savings accounts, Money Market accounts, short-term Certificates of Deposit, Treasury Bills, and savings bonds. These assets are generally short-term investments and can be considered emergency funds or "mad money".

The **debt** category represents fixed income investments designed to provide you with current income with relative stability of investment principle. Your investment dollars generally stay put while they yield "wages" or income from your principle. Investments in this category include: Treasury Notes, Treasury Bonds, municipal bonds, long-term certificates of deposit, fixed annuities, corporate bonds, and bond mutual funds. The duration of these investments ranges from one to thirty years. Fixed income investments tend to be most prosperous in times of a slow or declining economy and are most appropriate for those nearing retirement.

The **equity** category of investments implies ownership; it represents the opposite of debt. The equity investor shares in the wealth and/or risk as they are created, and has certain rights like inspecting balance sheets. Equity investments include stocks, stock market mutual funds, and real estate. They should be considered long-term investments — at least two or three years in duration. This category provides for the growth necessary to protect against future inflation. Instability in the economy negatively impacts equity markets.

Asset Allocation: The Investment Matrix

Step Four in the process of securing your financial future will be to write your personal plan. Step Five will be to implement the plan. Finally, Step Six will be to monitor the plan on a regular, quarterly basis. Although you are not quite ready to do all of these at this point, I mention them here because we are about to examine an example that will take you through them.

Let's look at a sample investment matrix guided by the principles of Modern Portfolio Theory, to see what advantage we gain by properly balancing resources among the three investment categories. Remember, it is the mixing (diversification) of assets that will drive our returns.

Figure #11 outlines current and recommended allocations of investment dollars for Col. Dan D. Demo (my own John Doe) and the projected yield for each combination. If we jump ahead to look at the bottom line, you will note that the recommended combination of asset allocation resulted in nearly an 8.6% increase in the annual return on investments. To help you understand just how this was accomplished, however, go back to the beginning, and I will highlight the changes that were made in the investment categories.

On the first page of Figure #11, you will note that the reconfiguration of investment dollars includes dramatic increases in both the fixed income category and in stocks, and substantial decreases in cash/cash equivalents and property. The recommended allocation is a complete turn-around — placing 75% in fixed incomes and stocks.

The next two pages divide the Colonel's dollars into specific types of investments within larger categories, and provide a breakdown and total of annual returns. You will again notice dramatic increases. This time they are in investment returns. The bread and butter income from the "beefed up" investment categories emphatically supports the suggested shift in assets. And you are in it for the money, aren't you?

The final page of Figure #11 gives a long-term analysis of investment income and a schedule for quarterly review, underscoring the cyclical nature of the financial picture and the need to stay abreast of the cycle.

Figure #11
Asset Allocation Sample

ASSET ALLOCATION

Investment Categories	Current Asset Allocation	Recommended Asset Allocation
Cash/Cash Equivalents	286,186	42,215-
Fixed Income	142,059	422,162+
Stocks	37,578	211,081+
Property Ownership	378,000	168,865-
Tangible Assets	500	0-
TOTALS:	$844,323	$844,323

PERCENTAGE ALLOCATION

Investment Categories	Current Asset Allocation	Recommended Asset Allocation
Cash/Cash Equivalents	33.90%	5.00%
Fixed Income	16.83%	50.00%
Stocks	4.45%	25.00%
Property Ownership	44.76%	20.00%
Tangible Assets	0.06%	0.00%
TOTALS:	100.00%	100.00%

The single most important dimension of investment policy is asset mix, particularly the ratio of fixed-income investments to equity investments.

Bradley Gummow

CURRENT ASSET ALLOCATION

Investments	Amount	Taxable Income	Non-Taxable Income
Cash/Cash Equivalents			
Money Markets	85,885	3,435	
Tax-Free Money Markets	33,289		1,165
Certificates of Deposit	96,995	5,819	
Savings Accounts	70,017	3,326	
TOTAL	$286,186		
Fixed Income			
Municipal Bonds	96,450		6,269
Managed Bond Funds	31,863	2,868	
IRA Government Securities	13,746		
TOTAL	$142,059		
Stocks			
Stocks	10,666	373	
IRA Stock Funds	15,114		
IRA Growth Funds	11,798		
TOTAL	$378,000		
Property Ownership			
Rental-Park City	255,000	12,500	
Rental-St. George	63,000	1,400	
Rental-California	60,000	1,200	
TOTAL	$378,000		
Tangible Assets			
Gold Fund	500		
TOTAL	$500		
Earned Income		75,000	
Pensions		44,980	
TOTAL ASSETS	$844,323		
TOTAL INCOME		$150,901	$7,434
TOTAL ANNUAL INCOME		$158,335	

61

RECOMMENDED ASSET ALLOCATION

Investments	Amount	Taxable Income	Non-Taxable Income
Cash/Cash Equivalents			
Tax-Free Money Markets	12,215		428
Certificates of Deposit	30,000	1,800	
TOTAL	$42,215		
Fixed Income			
Municipal Bonds	176,450		11,469
Managed Bond Funds	150,000	12,000	
Zero-Coupon Bonds*	30,000		
IRA Government Securities	13,746		
TOTAL	$370,196		
Stocks			
Managed Equity Funds	150,000	15,000	
IRA Blue-Chip Stock Fund	26,912		
TOTAL	$176,912		
Property Ownership			
Rental-Park City	255,000	12,500	
TOTAL	$255,000		
Earned Income		75,000	
Pensions		44,980	
TOTAL ASSETS	$844,323		
TOTAL INCOME		$161,280	$11,897
TOTAL ANNUAL INCOME		$173,177	

62

Bradley Gummow

FUTURE VALUE AND INCOME ANALYSIS

Investments	Rates of Return	Amount	Years	
			5	7
Municipal Bonds	6.50%	176,450	241,752	274,201
Managed Bond Fund	8.00%	150,000	220,399	257,074
Managed Equity Fund	10.00%	150,000	241,577	292,308
Rental-Park City	6.00%	255,000	341,248	383,426
Zero-Coupon Bond	8.00%	30,000	44,080	51,415
IRA Gov't Securities	8.00%	13,746	20,197	23,558
IRA B-C Stk Fund	10.00%	26,912	43,342	52,444
TOTAL		$802,108	$1,152,594	$1,334,425
ANNUAL INCOME		$63,768	$91,631	$106,087
DISCOUNTED FUTURE VALUE		$802,108	$947,348	$1,014,053
DISCOUNTED INCOME		$63,768	$75,314	$80,617

Future values assume income at rates of return shown is reinvested. Income at any given year assumes no income taken in previous years. Discounted Future Value and Income assume 4.00% inflation. Rates of return are based on past performance and reflect no indication of guarantee of future performance.

PORTFOLIO REVIEW SCHEDULE
October 1, 1998
January 1, 1999
April 1, 1999
July 1, 1999

63

Now that you have examined a workable allocation of investment dollars, get out your completed Worksheet #6 and have a look at your allocation. How does it compare? If you find it lacking in light of what you have learned, don't lose heart. Remember: You are the architect. If you don't like that plan, you have the power to draw another one. You are building the skills to turn that hodgepodge into a productive combination of complementary parts.

As I discuss the specific types of investments in more depth in the chapters that follow, you will develop a keener perspective on each of them. This will enhance your ability to match investments to your particular objectives and achieve the proper balance for optimum return on your dollars.

Investment Risks

Risk is a crucial determining factor when comparing investment options. Defined simply, risk is the chance of loss. Investment risk takes many forms. An understanding of the various types of risk will enable you to consider their impact on the different categories of investment.

In general, the higher the potential profit or yield from an investment, the greater the amount of risk. America's national pastime provides a perfect illustration of this point. Babe Ruth is the number two homerun hitter of all time. "The Babe" is, however, ranked number one in all-time strikeouts. The batter who goes for the base hits usually has a higher batting average than the homerun hitter. He scores runs; it just takes a bit longer. In other words, the risk in the investment field can be compared to the risk on the baseball field. Big swings bring big hits…or big misses.

In this section, I will discuss each of the following five types of investment risk: inflation/yield, interest rate, credit, market, and liquidity.

Inflation/Yield Risk. This is the risk of having the purchasing power of your principle eroded through inflation, and the risk of having the income from an investment rise and fall with market rates of interest. If you've invested in CD's, Treasury Bills, or Money-Market funds, you have always been subject to it. While the Federal Deposit Insurance Corporation protects your CD investments, there is no guarantee on the rate of inflation.

To protect yourself from inflation/yield risk, you need to invest at least part of your portfolio in equities (such as stocks or real estate). To help alleviate the effect of fluctuating interest rates, vary your CD or Treasury Bill maturity dates.

Interest-Rate Risk. This is the possibility that interest rates will rise after you've acquired your investment. The effect of such a post-purchase rise, of course, would be to make the fixed rate of interest on your investment (6%, for example) less attractive relative to the higher rates (8%, for example) that an investor could get on a new, but otherwise similar investment. In 1972, many thought it was a sweet deal when they locked in their CD's at 6%. But what happened right after that? Interest rates went through the roof, and we experienced the highest rates of all time.

If you invest today in long-term bonds or other interest-bearing investments, you're accepting a great deal of interest-rate risk because interest rates are currently low and likely to rise in the future. If you decide to buy bonds, you can reduce your interest-rate risk by buying bonds with shorter terms.

Credit Risk. Companies and municipalities having a higher risk of default must pay more to borrow money than those with better credit ratings. For example, if we started a company right now — say, XYZ Manufacturing --— we would have to pay more to borrow money than

AT&T who has an established track record. If your bond fund is quoting rates much higher than you can get in a safer investment, find out how much risk of default you're accepting.

If your fund is investing in high-risk bonds, you're at a risk of losing your principal or having your yield drop in the event of default. If you want to safeguard your investment dollars, consider the credit rating factor.

Market Risk. If you invest in stocks or in mutual funds that invest in stocks, you'll be subject to market risk. This is the risk associated with fluctuations in the stock market, and your portfolio or mutual fund in particular.

You can minimize market risk by investing small amounts over a long period of time (dollar-cost averaging) and by buying the stocks of several different companies (diversification).

Liquidity Risk. Liquidity is the ease with which an investment can be sold. An investment that cannot be sold easily is said to be illiquid. If you're considering investing in a limited partnership, real estate, or collectibles (art, antiques, jewelry, etc.), you may not be able to sell your investment quickly if you need cash.

Keep liquidity in mind in deciding where to invest. Tangible investments (like coins, precious metals, art, and collectibles) are at their best in times of rampant inflation and random political events. Since emergencies cannot necessarily be scheduled to coincide with these conditions, it would be wise to consider other types of investments for money you may need in the short-term.

To help you visualize the interaction of risk and rate of return, I have constructed a simple graph. Figure #12 — Standard Deviation locates the rate of investment return on one axis and the risk factor on the other.

Figure #12
Risk/Return Standard Deviation

Standard Deviation is a measure of the risk associated with an investment. This chart illustrates how global
investing (with a 75% equity and 25% bond matrix) provided less risk than the Standard & Poor's 500, and still
produced a handsome return.

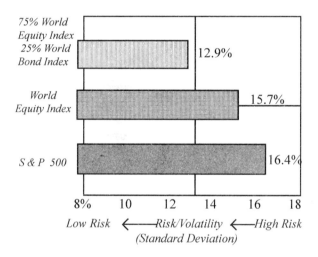

Sources: G.T. Capital Management, Inc.; Morgan Stanley
Capital International; Salomon Bros. Past experience does
not assure future results and performance of indices may
not correlate with the performance of your investments.
Figures represent the 10-year period ended December 31,
1991.

Optimistically, we desire to be in the upper left corner where we achieve the highest rate of return possible, with the least volatility. Realistically speaking, however, we recognize that we aren't going to get the highest rate of return without some type of risk. Yet, we don't want to turn our investment portfolio into a casino of sorts, do we?

How do we reconcile the risk/return factors? Again, duration and diversity in our investments will help balance these. You have already looked at a variety of factors such as dependability, duration, and tax brackets for guidance in investment decisions. As you evaluate specific types of investments for your personal portfolio, consider the risk factor in weighing their merits.

11 Investment Mistakes to Avoid

Open nearly any newspaper or business magazine, and you'll be flooded with tips on how to invest and what to buy. But dodging investment pitfalls is a crucial part of choosing the right place for your dollars. The October 1992 issue of *Fact* magazine lists ten tempting, but most often misguided investment approaches. My experience in the field leads me to add an eleventh.

1) ***Acting on hot tips.*** Although it is tempting to buy stocks on rumors of mergers or new products, be aware that the stock price might already reflect the rumors.
2) ***Following crowds.*** Highly touted stocks have already risen sharply. Out-of-favor stocks can be a better bet.
3) ***Failure to see investment risk.*** For example, note that interest-rate swings affect bond values, and that limited partnerships and small company stocks are often illiquid.
4) ***Buying for tax advantages.*** Tax benefits add luster

68

to an investment, but profit should be your main goal.

5) *Failure to keep tabs.* Even if you own a mutual fund, be sure it owns securities you're comfortable with.

6) *Failure to take profits.* Don't get greedy, and don't be afraid to sell when a stock is still hot. Consider cashing in part of your investment if you're unsure.

7) *Failure to take losses.* Don't sit on a bad investment. If you don't have reason to expect a turn around, pull your money out and invest somewhere else.

8) *Failure to diversify.* Owning a variety of investments limits the pain if any one investment turns sour.

9) *Investing on reflex.* You could be chasing yesterday's bargain by reacting to tips in the news. But remember: Truly good advice is valid both now and later.

10) *Lack of discipline.* If you don't have a steady regimen for investing, check out mutual funds or money managers who follow a strategy that meets your needs.

11) *Acting on sentiment.* The company that gave you your first job or built your first car may deserve a special place in your heart, but not in your investment plan. Earning trends, not company names are important in choosing where to invest.

Chapter 3

Cash/Cash Equivalents and Fixed Income

"It is better to have a permanent income than to be fascinating."

Oscar Wilde

Cash/Cash Equivalents

While the Japanese save anywhere from 15-22% of their income, we Americans tend to save between 1 1/2% and 6%, depending on our stage in the economic cycle. (I apologize for indulging in the overused format of American/Japanese economic comparison, but it has been such a ripe area in modern times, and it illustrates my point.) How does that impact our individual future financial outlook?

Let's project some figures for an income of $40,000. If you put away 7% ($2,800 annually) and earn an 8% rate of return, you will have $141,184 in twenty years. Was that so hard? All you had to do was put away about $54.00 per week. I've said it before, and I'll continue to drive the point home: the process for accumulating wealth is no mystery. It involves, quite simply, the efficient, well-executed investment plan you are learning to build here.

The first investment category we will explore in detail is Cash/Cash Equivalents and Fixed Income. It includes both short and long-term vehicles; those with a fixed rate of return and those with growth potential. Depending on your age bracket and your investment style, the combined elements of this category could make up anywhere between 30-70% of your matrix. In the chapter on putting together your plan, I will discuss more specifically how your age and stage in life impact your matrix; suffice it to say at this point that the percentage invested in this category will increase as your age increases.

Cash investments include, obviously, funds that are available to you immediately. Cash equivalents are those that can be converted to cash in a year or less without much market risk. Money market funds and certificates of deposit are examples of these. Cash and cash equivalents should be considered short-term investments that will "underwrite" your emergencies or unanticipated but necessary expenditures. In most instances, you should have less money invested this way than in fixed income vehicles, and as you get older, this portion of the category should actually increase.

Many of our parents and grandparents equated savings with a savings account. Whatever cash was not required to fulfill the basic and immediate needs of the family went into the bank — or the mattress for those who were less confident in financial institutions. The modern investment portfolio, however, does not usually include these. Why not? In the case of the bedding account, the answer is obvious. In the case of the traditional savings account the interest rate or return on your investment, historically only keeps pace with inflation 60% of the time.

Money market accounts and certificates of deposit can generate the return on your investment that old-fashioned passbook accounts fail to deliver. Figure #13, A Guide to Available Money Market Instruments, will help you evaluate the merits of a variety of potential money market investments. It provides information on guarantor, marketability, duration, denomination, and basis for return. Please note the use of the lower case "m" to designate the $1,000 denomination and "mm" to denote $1,000,000. The Roman numeral, rather than the "k" used in engineering, is the standard financial term.

U.S. Treasury Bills (T-Bills) are regarded as the single safest investment in the world. They are backed by the "full faith and credit of the United States government" — a powerful guarantee based on taxing power. Since our federal government has such excellent credit, the secondary market for Treasury Bills is excellent. Recalling our discussion of risk at the end of Chapter 2, T-Bills are excellent risks with respect to liquidity and credit. Not all money market investments carry the same guarantee as T-Bills. Make sure you examine and understand the parameters of each type before you decide which ones best suit your portfolio.

It is also important to note that federal agency is not synonymous with the federal government. The Federal Deposit Insurance Corporation (FDIC) is an example of an agency created by the government that independently insures deposits in banks, like certificates of deposit, checking accounts, and NOW accounts. While investments backed by the FDIC are relatively low risk, the FDIC does not have the "full faith and credit" of the United States Government behind it.

In addition to the risk factor, you must also consider a number of other factors impacting the performance of your money market investments. The interest rates on these investments are affected by various activities in the economic cycle. Figure #14, How Significant Indicators Affect Interest Rates, outlines three areas that forecast movement of interest rates: monetary policy of the Federal Reserve, inflation and business activities. Careful monitoring of your investments includes attention to these factors.

The Federal Reserve Board, currently chaired by Alan Greenspan, is an agency of the Treasury Department run by a board of governors. Their job is to oversee the amount of money in circulation in the United States. They are the ones who basically control interest rates and the fed or discount rate. Interest rates were lowered twenty-three times in a row in an attempt to ignite our economy. That is an all-time record for a capitalist, as I far as I know. The Bundes Bank, the German counterpart of our Federal Reserve, has recently begun to lower interest rates for the same reason we did. When inflation began rearing its ugly here, the Fed raised interest rates.

Gold prices are a fairly reliable indicator of the movement of interest rates. Can you recall the price of gold in 1979 and 1980? It was nearly three times the current price. Guess what else was three times higher. That's right, interest rates. Industrial uses aside, the price of gold is generally a good barometer of interest rate direction.

The Consumer Price Index (CPI) provides clues to the movement of inflation. If the CPI rises, look for inflation to rear its ugly head. As the demand for products increases, so does the price, and we can generally expect inflation to follow suit.

Business activity will affect interest rates on certificates of deposit and on bonds, which I will discuss next. An increase in housing starts, for example, usually signals growth in the economy. As a result, interest rates will eventually increase. If the government index of leading economic indicators signals an extremely healthy economy, the price of goods and services will increase. What goes up as a result? Interest rates. Then there is a slow down in the economy resulting in increased unemployment. Since unemployed people do not spend as much, demand for goods and services cycle down, and prices must follow.

Heeding the factors that impact interest rates helps the investor maximize returns. Monitoring and making adjustments in your portfolio at appropriate times in the economic cycle, is essential to keeping your dollars working for you.

Figure #13

A GUIDE TO AVAILABLE MONEY MARKET INSTRUMENTS

1) *United States Treasury Bills*

Obligation - U.S. Gov't obligation. U.S. Treasury auctions 3 & 6 month bills weekly. Also offers through special auctions, 1 year maturities and tax anticipation series.
Marketability - Excellent secondary market.
Maturities - Up to 1 year.
Denomination - 10m to 1mm. (5m multiples after first 10m.)
Basis - Discounted. Actual days on a 360-day basis.

2) *U.S. Treasury Notes & Bonds*

Obligation - U.S. Gov't obligation.
Marketability - Excellent secondary market.
Maturities - Notes up to 10 years. Bonds unlimited.
Denomination - 1m to 10mm.
Basis - Yield basis on a 365-day year semi-annual interest.

3) *Federal Agencies*

Obligation - Various agencies established by Congress. Obligations are sole responsibility of issuing body. With few exceptions the U.S. Gov't assumes no liability.
Marketability - Excellent secondary market.
Maturities - Various maturities up to and longer than one year.
Denomination - 1m/5m/10m/1mm
Basis - Generally on yield basis 30-day month on 360-day year. Most issues carry coupon.

4) *Direct Sales Finance Paper*

> Obligation - Promissory notes of finance companies placed directly with the investor through commercial paper dealers.
> Marketability - No secondary market. Companies under certain conditions will buy back paper prior to maturity. Many will adjust rate.
> Maturities - Issued to mature on any day from 3 to 270 days.
> Denomination - 25m to 5mm.
> Basis - Discounted or interest-bearing. Actual days on a 360-day year.

5) *Dealer Paper: A)Finance, B)Industrial*

> Obligation - Promissory notes of finance companies and leading industrial firms sold through commercial paper dealers.
> Marketability - No secondary market. Buy back arrangement can usually be negotiated through the dealer.
> Maturities - 1) Issued to mature from 3 to 270 days. 2) Available on certain dates between 30 and 180 days.
> Denomination - 100m to 5mm.
> Basis - Discounted. Actual days on a 360-day year.

6) *Banker's Acceptances*

> Obligation - Time draft drawn on and accepted by a banking institution, which is credit for that of the holder or importer of the merchandise.
> Marketability - Good secondary market.
> Maturities - Up to 6 months.
> Denomination - 25m to 1mm.
> Basis - Discounted. Actual days on a 360-day basis.

7) *Negotiable Time*

> Obligation - Certificates of Time Deposit at a commercial bank.
> Marketability - Limited secondary market.
> Maturities - Usually up to 1 year, occasionally longer.
> Denomination - 100m to 5mm.
> Basis - Yield basis. Actual days on a 360-day year. Interest at maturity.

8) *Repurchase Agreement (REPO)*

> Obligation - Sale of securities with a simultaneous commitment to repurchase after a predetermined period of time at a specified rate of interest.
> Marketability - No secondary market.
> Maturities - Overnight to 30 days, occasionally longer.
> Denomination - 100m and up.
> Basis - Interest-bearing. Actual days on a 360-day basis.

9) *Federal Funds*

> Obligation - An unsecured transaction with the funds returned to the seller with interest at maturity.
> Marketability - No secondary market.
> Maturities - Generally overnight, occasionally longer.
> Denomination - 100m and up.
> Basis - Interest bearing. Actual days on a 360-day basis.

Figure #14

HOW SIGNIFICANT INDICATORS AFFECT INTEREST RATES

The Federal Reserve and Monetary Policy

INDICATOR

1) Money supply figures: M-1 cash in circulation, checking NOW accts, mutual savings; M-2 plus money market accts, time deposits, overnight repos, overnight Euros.

> Release Date - Each Thursday, 4:30 EST.
> Effect - Money supply goes up; yields up.
> Reasons - Excess growth in money causes inflation and fear that Fed will tighten.

2) Fed buying bills.

> Effect - Yields down.
> Reasons - Fed adds money to system.

3) Fed tightening.

> Effect - Yields up.
> Reasons - Fed fears growth in money supply. Fed funds may rise with other short-term rates.

4) Fed doing repos.

> Effect - Yields down.
> Reasons - Fed puts money in system by purchasing securities & agreeing to resell; increase money supply.

5) Fed doing reverse or match sales.

> Effect - Yields up.
> Reasons - Fed takes money out of system by selling securities & agreeing to repurchase: decrease money supply.

6) Fed raises discount rate.

> Effect - Yields up.
> Reasons - Increase in rates between Fed & member banks means increase in customer loss rates; used to slow inflation.

7) Increase in anticipated bond supply.

> Release Date - Reported in financial press each Monday.
> Effect - Yields up.
> Reasons -Indicates greater demand for credit.

INFLATION

1) Consumer price index is up.

> Release Date - Late in month for prior month.
> Effect - Yields up.
> Reasons - Inflationary.

2) Product price index is up. Rise.

> Release Date - First week for prior month.
> Effect - Yields up.
> Reasons - Demands for goods inflation indicator.

BUSINESS ACTIVITY

1) GNP is down.

> Release Date - Quarterly revision at mid-month.
> Effect - Yields down.
> Reasons - Slowing economy; Fed may loosen by allowing rates to go down.

2) Housing starts up.

> Release Date - Mid-month for prior month.
> Effect - Yields up.
> Reasons - Growth in economy with new housing demand for goods & mortgages rise. Fed may tighten.

3) Industrial production down.

> Release Date - Mid-month for prior month.
> Effect - Yields down.
> Reasons - Inventory levels good indicators of duration & intensity of business slow-down.

4) Leading indicators up.

> Release Date - Late in month for prior month.
> Effect - Yields up.
> Reasons - Leading indicators are advance signals about health of economy.

5) Personal income up.

> Release Date - Late in month for prior month.
> Effect - Yields up.
> Reasons - The higher your income, the more you consume, leading to more demand & higher prices; inflationary.

6) Retail sales up.

> Release Date - Mid-month for prior month.
> Effect - Yields up.
> Reasons - Indication of economic growth; Fed may tighten.

7) Trade balance up.

> Release Date - Late in month for prior month.
> Effect - Yields up.
> Reasons - Dollar strengthens, anticipates foreign demand.

8) Unemployment up.

> Release Date - First Friday for prior month.
> Effect - Yields down.
> Reasons - High unemployment indicates lack of expansion in economy.

Fixed Income: Bond Basics

Investors seeking greater capital security and assured income often invest in corporate or government bonds. They are labeled fixed income investments because the return on bonds is a specific, fixed rate paid at regular intervals, and the maximum return in a known or fixed quantity.

A bond represents a loan to the issuer; it is a debt that must be paid. The bond issuer agrees to repay the amount borrowed plus a specified rate of interest at an agreed time, the maturity date. Bondholders are creditors rather than part-owners or shareholders of a company. The bond certificate lists the following: the name of the issuer, a serial number, the principal amount of the bond, the rate of interest, and the maturity (repayment) date. In addition, provisions may be made for a bond to be purchased back by the issuer (subject to call) at a stated price before the maturity date.

In most cases, a bond owner cannot expect to receive more from the issuer than the amount stated in the bond agreement, regardless of how the company may prosper. Bond interest is paid much in the same way as interest on a savings account. It accrues daily, and you earn income for only the days you own the bond. If you own a bond for ninety days out of a given year at 9%, you will receive no more, no less than ninety days of 9% interest. In other words, bonds are not growth investments.

How does bond ownership compare to stock investment? I will outline a few distinct differences here and you will gain even more specific insight from the next chapter on stocks. One factor that may influence your choice between bonds and stocks is position in the payment hierarchy. Before a company can pay dividends to stockholders, they must make interest payments to bondholders. If the bond issuer should liquidate or go bankrupt, bondholders' claims must be satisfied before stockholders.

Bonds have a lower risk factor than stocks. A bond is a promise to pay a debt, and the face amount of the bond is guaranteed at maturity. Inflation may affect the power of your dollars by the time the bond matures, but you will, in any case, get back what you paid. For the seller, bond prices fluctuate with interest rates; but the interest rate on a specific bond is locked in.

Bondholders can expect a steady income from bonds. Depending on your age and stage, these fixed income vehicles may make up 10%-65% of your investment matrix. The percentage of your investment in bonds will generally increase with age, and they will constitute the majority of your investment dollars during your retirement years. Regular payments at the fixed interest rate are made by creditworthy issuers. Stocks yield growth, returns may not materialize until they are sold.

Due to a reciprocal agreement between our federal government and local governing bodies, some bonds have tax-exempt status. The federal government does not tax individuals on municipal bond income, and the state does not tax income on federal bond income. As you keep an eye on your marginal tax bracket, this may have a significant impact on the choice between municipal bonds and taxable bonds.

While bonds are considered fixed income, and your entire principal investment will be returned to you at maturity, bond prices fluctuate in the market. You should, in the wise exercise of your investment plan, monitor these prices, and you may want to reconfigure your bond investments in light of changes in interest rates and bond values. If the interest on your bond does not stay ahead of inflation over the long haul, your purchasing power erodes. (Bonds are long-term investments, so don't forget the big picture — view the cycle rather than minor or uncharacteristic changes.) Even if you get all your dollars back at maturity, they may be worth less than when you invested them, in terms of purchasing power. Ah, inflation!

Why do bond prices fluctuate? Like all securities, they bend to the forces of supply and demand. The level of investors' faith in the issue is a fundamental influence on bond prices. However, forces behind the shifts in supply and demand exert more pressure on interest rates in the overall credit markets.

Bonds are initially sold in $1,000 denominations. They can be sold by the bond purchaser at whatever price the market will bear at the time of sale, but at maturity, they return the initial $1,000 to the current bond owner. Since the interest rate on a bond is fixed, the income earned (current yield) is relative to the price paid for the bond. For example, if you paid $990 for a bond with a 5% interest rate, your yield would be 5.05% on that investment. If you paid $1,100 for that same bond, your yield would be 4.55%. Bond value will act in an inverse relationship to current interest rates. Since the interest rate on a bond is locked in for the duration, as interests rise, bond values decline. As interest rates exceed current bond yields, demand tends to shift away from the bond market into the credit (bank) market. Bondholders will then sell their bonds to move their funds, thus creating downward pressure of the bond prices.

At some point in the interest rate cycle, the value (return on the dollar investment) in the bond market will either equal or exceed the value in credit markets and prices will start to rise again.

Evaluation of a bond investment must take into consideration the issue price of the bond, the current price, and the interest rates in the variety of investment markets. The impact of government fiscal policy — taxing and spending — and actions of the Federal Reserve Board must also be factored into the formula before an accurate return on your investment dollars can be calculated.

Bond Quality

The quality rating of a bond is an important consideration in the process of your bond investment decision. Bond ratings are assigned by independent ranking agencies and can range from AAA (triple A), the highest possible rating, to D, for default. The premier bond-rating agency is Standard and Poor's; among the other respected rating agencies are Moody's and Duff and Phelps.

The AAA rating is generally reserved for the federal government and the strongest, well-established U.S. corporations. Only a handful of U.S. corporations have earned an AAA status. Other ratings include AA, A, BBB, BB, B and so on through the dreaded D. A defaulted bond is generally a bond that has stopped paying interest because the company has run into financial difficulty. For obvious reasons, the "D" rating usually results in a dramatic drop in the value of the bond.

The term "junk bond" became a very popular phrase in the press, painting what I think is a broad and misleading picture of something that requires closer examination.

84

It is a generally accepted rule in the investment business to consider BBB-rated bonds as the cut-off point for investment-grade bonds. In other words, you can feel relatively comfortable with bonds rated BBB or higher, although more conservative investors may not consider anything below AA. The junk category, then, encompasses the BB-rating and below. Junk bonds may result in higher yield, but surely you remember the relationship between risk and yield.

Junk bonds are sometimes divided into an upper and lower tier. In my opinion, BB and B-rated bonds constitute the upper tier, and there are a number of opportunities there if you exercise due caution. The lower tier is comprised of CCC-rated bonds and lower; these are generally regarded as the true "junk" bonds.

The Variety of Bonds

Literally thousands of bonds are available to investors. The United States Government and its agencies, state and local governments and business corporations issue bonds. Here is a listing and brief description of the principle types of bonds you might include in your investment portfolio.

Marketable United States Government Bonds. The federal government constantly borrows, mostly through long-term bonds. Since the government has the highest credit rating of any borrower, its bonds are considered the safest. It can usually borrow at lower rates than other entities or individuals. Dealers maintain an active market in U.S. bonds, many of which can be purchased on the New York Stock Exchange.

Tax-Exempt Bonds. Billions of dollars worth of bonds are issued by American state and local government units. All bonds of this type issued by public units of government are called municipal bonds. These may include municipalities, school districts, sanitary districts, fire protection districts, and water districts. An advantage of municipal bonds is their federal income tax-exempt status, although capital gains on them may be subject to taxation. In addition, nearly every state or city that levies income and personal property tax exempts its resident-owned bonds or that of its subdivisions, such as municipalities or school districts.

Municipal bonds also offer relative safety of principal, rating only second to federal obligations. Like all securities, however, they have varying risks. In some cases, very few however, municipals have declined substantially, and some defaults have occurred.

Corporate Issues. Among corporate borrowing, the terms of bonds agreements vary substantially. As a general rule, a corporate bond issue has a set maturity date. Sometimes a corporation will agree to have a given number of its bonds mature annually over a number of years, rather than all at once. These are called "sinking fund" bonds.

Convertibles. An interesting feature of some bond contracts is the privilege of converting the bond into a specified number of shares of a company's common stock. This option changes the characteristic of the bond by allowing growth potential. There are three advantages to the convertible type of bond. First, those who hold them are entitled to interest payments before common and preferred stockholders are paid. Next, they offer potential price appreciation linked to the company's earnings. Finally, they provide some of the stability associated with regular bonds and preferred stock.

When the issuing company's stock price goes up, the conversion privilege becomes more valuable. As the price raises, the bond acts more like a stock and less like a bond. Conversely, if the company's stock price falls, the conversion feature loses advantage, and the bond price ɩy also decline.

GNMA Bonds

Today, you don't have to sacrifice quality for yield, thanks to a growing list of mortgage securities.

Mortgage-collateralized with Government National Mortgage Association (GNMA or Ginnie Mae) Modified Pass Through Certificates are among the most attractive. Timely payment of principal and interest is guaranteed by the full faith and credit of the U.S. Government so the underlying safety is the responsibility of the federal agency and not the issuer.

Eight Key Reasons for Considering GNMA-Backed Bonds

Yield. GNMA-backed bonds have ranged from 5.75% to 8.75% during the past several years, generally one-half of a percent higher than 10-year Government bonds.

$10,000 Denominations. This low minimum purchase of $10,000 (generally) is ideally suited to investors with excess funds in money market accounts, maturing certificates of deposit or bonds, and funds generated from IRA or Keogh plans.

Safety. The GNMA's, the underlying collateral, are held by an independent bank trustee on behalf of bondholders. The GNMA-backed bonds are rated AAA by Standard & Poor's.

Monthly Income. Because no principle is returned until redemption, you will receive the same amount of interest each month for each $1,000 bond.

Death Redemption. If an individual or jointly registered bondholder dies, the estate or survivor will have priority redemption privileges.

Put Feature. In many cases, bondholders may put

their bonds to the Trustee for redemption, up to $10,000 per month, per bondholder.

Call Protection. Bondholders are afforded six-year call protection unless the underlying mortgages begin rapid repayment and, consequently, reduce the flow of interest to the Trustee. In such a case, the Trustee is required to randomly call bonds or call the entire issuer at face value to protect the principal and interest of bondholders.

Government Agency obligations are not guaranteed by the Federal Government but they are considered relatively free of risk. They are traded in a broad, active secondary market in which settlement can be effected as expeditiously as for Treasury Bills. Moreover, agency securities are treated as non-risk assets for examination purposes and may be pledged to secure Treasury Tax and Loan Account balances, and security for advances by the Federal Reserve to member banks.

The Federal National Mortgage Association (FNMA or Fannie Mae) is a government sponsored corporation owned entirely by private stockholders to serve as a secondary market for Federal Housing Administration, Veteran's Administration, or Farmer's Home Administration insured or guaranteed mortgages. The association provides liquidity on mortgage investments by buying mortgages when normal funds are in short supply and selling mortgages when funds are plentiful. Fannie Maes come in book entry form only with a minimum of $10,000 and increments of $5,000 thereafter. The maturity on these securities varies. Interest is paid monthly and is subject to Federal taxes. However, there is no specific exemption for state and local taxes.

The following bonds are all United States Government guaranteed as to payment of principal and total interest. They are legal investments for commercial banks, insurance companies and various fiduciary and trust funds. Also, they're eligible to secure public funds and as collateral for Treasury Tax and Loan Accounts. They are subject to Federal Income Tax.

U.S. Treasury Securities

Treasury Bills are issued at a discount through an auction inviting tenders for competitive and noncompetitive bidding ($500,000 maximum for noncompetitive orders). Bills are in book entry form only and are paid at face amount without interest at maturity. The difference between price and maturity value is considered an ordinary interest income. This income is subject to all federal taxes and exempt from state and local taxes. Treasury bills come in a minimum of $10,000 with $5,000 denominations thereafter.

3 and 6 Month Bills are normally auctioned weekly on Monday with settlement the following Thursday, (these days are subject to holidays).

52 Week Bills are auctioned every four weeks on Thursday with settlement the following Thursday.

Cash Management Bills are auctioned occasionally to fill the gap in Government spending and tax dates. Usually they mature within a few days after auction. Minimum denominations of $10,000.

Treasury Notes may be issued with a maturity of not less than one year or more than 10 years, with varying denominations due to maturities. Notes can be book entry or registered. Treasury notes originate through auctions with competitive and noncompetitive bidding ($1,000,000 maximum for noncompetitive orders). Interest is paid semi-annually and is subject to federal taxes but exempt from state local taxes.

2 Year Notes are auctioned every month. They are dated and mature as of month's end. $5,000 denominations.

3 Year Notes are auctioned as part of the Quarterly

Refunding Package in February, May, August, and November. They are dated and mature in said month on the 15th. $5,000 denominations.

4 Year Notes are auctioned early in the last month of every quarter. They are dated and mature at month's end. $1,000 denominations.

5 Year Notes have been auctioned payable in early March, June, September, and December. $1,000 denominations.

7 & 10 Year Notes are each used as an option in the Quarterly Refunding Package. One or the other is chosen to suit present needs. They are dated and mature on the 15th of said month.

Treasury Bonds may be issued with a maturity of over 10 years. $1,000 denominations. Bonds can be book entry or registered. Treasury bonds originate through auctions with competitive and noncompetitive bidding. ($1,000,000 maximum for noncompetitive bidding). Interest is paid semi-annually and is subject to federal taxes but exempt from state and local taxes.

15 Year Bonds are auctioned in January, April, July, and October. They are dated and mature on the 15th of said month.

25- to 30-Year Bonds are auctioned as part of the Quarterly Refunding Package. They are dated and mature on the 15th of said month.

The Farmer's Home Administration is an agency of the United States Department of Agriculture that furnishes supervised credit and management and credit advice to farmers and other rural families that are unable to get sufficient credit from any other source at reasonable rates and terms, to finance actual needs in farming, housing, and development of new small enterprises to increase low family income. The certificates are issuable in coupon or registered form, denominations of $25,000, $50,000, $100,000, $500,000, and $1,000,000.

Government National Mortgage Association Pass Throughs are V.A. and F.H.A. mortgage-backed securities. Ginnie Maes come in registered form only, (no certificates issued). Interest is paid monthly. The timely payment of principal and interest is backed by the Federal Government. Ginnie Maes offer investors an opportunity to participate in high yielding "pools" of government guaranteed or insured mortgages without having to be concerned with the extensive documentation and paper work associated with mortgage type investments.

CMO Investments

In 1983, the introduction of Collateralized Mortgage Obligations (CMO's) by the Federal Home Loan Mortgage Corporation established a new investment vehicle for investors not traditionally involved in the mortgage market. CMO's transformed standard thirty-year mortgages into obligations comprised of several different classes or tranches designed to appeal to a broad range of investors. The Tax Reform Act of 1986 authorized the establishment of REMIC's which provided monthly pay possibilities to investors and a tax advantage to issuers. For investment purposes, REMIC securities are indistinguishable from CMO's. Today, virtually all CMO's issued are actually REMIC's. The CMO market has grown to over $250 billion in size since its inception in 1983 and today accounts for an ever increasing and important segment of the overall mortgage market.

What is a CMO? A CMO is a debt issue secured by pools of mortgages guaranteed by government agencies (GNMA, FNMA, or FHLMC) or private insurers and generally receives a AAA rating from rating agencies. The key feature which distinguishes a CMO from a standard Ginnie Mae or similar pass-through security, is the prioritization of the cash flow received from the mortgages and their distribution to several classes of bondholders. This mechanism creates a set of securities with various average life assumptions that are attractive to a variety of investors.

Each CMO is generally structured to have five to fifteen classes or tranches. CMO's receive principal payments from the pool of loans or securities collateralizing the issue of which are then allocated to each tranch according to the provisions set forth in the indenture. In addition to principal payments, investors receive interest payments (usually monthly) on the outstanding principal balance of their respective class of bonds. However, many CMO structures also include tranches known as Z bonds or Coupon Accural Bonds (CAB's) which, instead of paying out interest to the investor, add the accrued interest to the outstanding principal until principal payments begin. While similar to zero coupon bonds, CAB's are not sold at a discount but are generally offered at par with the accrued interest added to the principal balance.

What are the features of CMO's? CMO's enable investors to more closely match their requirements for maturity and timing of principal payments. Standard GNMA pass-through bonds have monthly principal payments which begin from the time of purchase with their effective maturities often hard to pinpoint. The tranch concept inherent in CMO's, gives investors looking for a particular maturity a better idea as to the timing and size of expected principal payments.

More importantly, the CMO structure offers holders of the longer term tranches a degree of protection from the prepayment risk that may be associated with other mortgage investments.

A final attraction for individual investors is the fact that most CMO's are available in $1,000 increments, far less than the required minimum of many mortgage-backed securities.

While CMO's generally offer more predictable principal payments, it is important to remember that timing of principal payments can only be estimated due to the nature of the underlying mortgage collateral. **Who issues CMO's?** CMO's are issued by both government agencies and private issuers. The Federal National Mortgage Association (FNMA) and Federal Home Loan Mortgage Corporation (FHLMC) issue CMO's which are direct obligations of their respective agencies. Private label CMO's are generally high-quality, AAA-rated securities. In order to qualify for the highest possible rating, CMO's must be fully collaterized, which means that the mortgage cash flows must be able to support the debt service to the bonds under any prepayment or interest rate scenario. Therefore, if the collateral does not consist of agency certificates (which include the agency guarantees), it must be insured against default by an AAA-rated insurance company. Once a CMO is issued, the collateral is held in trust by a third party custodial bank. Any financial failure by the issuer has no impact on the CMO bondholder since the collateral backing the CMO is completely separate from the issuing corporation and is either backed by an agency guarantee or private insurance. Hence, CMO's backed by government agencies have virtually no credit risk, while CMO's backed by private insurance accept the credit quality of the insurance company (generally AAA-rated).

Are all CMO's created equal? Until 1986 the majority of CMO's issued were created using a four-class sequential-pay structure. In this structure, all of the principal payments from the underlying mortgage collateral were paid to the first tranches until all bonds were completely retired. While the first classes were receiving interest and principal payments, the other classes were receiving only interest — their principal remained intact. After the first class was paid off, the second class would start receiving principal payments, etc., until all class were paid off. This sequential paydown of principal allowed the earlier classes to maintain shorter terms while the later classes enjoyed longer terms under a variety or prepayment scenarios.

In 1986, the mortgage-backed securities market was beginning to attract a variety of traditional fixed income investors due to high yields and excellent credit quality. Some of these investors, however, could not take on the uncertainty regarding the timing of principal payments. To address this, CMO developers created the planned amortization class (PAC). A PAC is a class that has a fixed principal payment schedule regardless of how fast or slow the underlying mortgages prepay. PAC bondholders have very little cash-flow uncertainty — only under extremely low or high prepayment rates — and as a result PAC's are priced more expensively (with lower yields).

In order to provide the PAC's with cash flow certainty, the other classes, in exchange for much higher yields, take on the additional cash flow uncertainty. These NON-PAC's (commonly referred to as Companion classes) are very appealing to individual investors who do not need the cash flow certainty that PAC's provide (see Figure #15 on page ##). Individual investors compose the largest percentage of Companion class buyers. In exchange for withstanding more uncertainty regarding principal payment, Companion class buyers are compensated in terms of higher yields (See Figure #15).

Another structural change is the CMO's now have 5 to 15 tranches or more. What this means to the investor is that each tranche is smaller today than it was years ago and therefore takes a shorter period to time to pay its principal back. For example, a plain sequential-pay CMO circa 1983 had three to four tranches — each was expected to pay down over a five to seven year period. Today, because there are so many tranches in each issue, it is now possible for tranches to pay off in as little as six months.

A typical paydown period is now two to five years (see payment windows in Figure #15).

The move from the sequential-pay structure of years ago to today's PAC/Companion structure has mixed implications for the investor. Sequential-pay tranches had less volatility regarding timing of principal payments and more call protection but the investor had to ensure long paydown periods and a higher degree of extension risk. Today's Companion classes have more volatility but investors enjoy a much higher yield. In addition, today's CMO's have smaller paydown periods and better extension protection than sequential-pay tranches.

Not all companion tranches are created equal either. Some have more call risk and/or extension risk than others. It is important to be aware of how your bond performs under different prepayment assumptions.

Figure #15

ILLUSTRATION OF PAC, COMPANION AND
SEQUENTIAL-PAY TRANCHES

PAC

FNMA 89-22-E

10-year Treasury Yield (PSA)	Average Life	Yield	Window
10% (150)	10.69	8.90	2/98 - 9/03
9% (175)	10.69	8.90	2/98 - 9/03
8% (190)	10.69	8.90	2/98 - 9/03
7% (250)	10.69	8.90	2/98 - 9/03
6% (275)	10.69	8.90	2/98 - 9/03

COMPANION

FNMA 89-22-K			
10-year Treasury Yield (PSA)	Average Life	Yield	Window
10% (150)	12.10	9.55	2/01 - 7/02
9% (175)	10.40	9.50	3/99 - 12/00
8% (190)	9.27	9.40	11/97 - 12/99
7% (250)	5.39	9.05	6/94 - 9/95
6% (275)	4.50	8.90	10/93 - 10/94

SEQUENTIAL - PAY

RYLAND 87-C			
10-year Treasury Yield (PSA)	Average Life	Yield	Window
10% (150)	11.40	9.35	9/98 - 12/03
9% (175)	10.00	9.30	7/97 - 4/02
8% (190)	9.29	9.10	12/96 - 5/01
7% (250)	7.20	9.05	5/95 - 10/98
6% (275)	6.56	9.00	11/94 - 1/98

How can a CMO be evaluated? What is prepayment speed? One of the most important issues associated with CMO investing is the evaluation of the mortgage prepayment experience. The Public Securities Association model (PSA) is an index which expresses the rate of prepayment of the underlying mortgages relative to the average rate experience of mortgage loans.

Changes in PSA experience will change the expected average life of each CMO class — with the exception of PAC tranches. This element adds a degree of uncertainty for investors seeking an exact maturity of their holdings. In addition, for any investor not buying at par, a change in the prepayment speed will change the CMO's yield, just as it does for other pass-through securities. The PSA level used for given CMO is dependent on the underlying collateral. Generally, the higher the coupon, the higher the PSA. A "street" consensus of 13 mortgage dealers is often used to determine a PSA for a given type of collateral.

What do average life and prepayment window mean for the investor? The effective maturity of a CMO tranche is its average life. This term refers to the estimated midpoint of the principal stream which will eventually retire the class. While principal cash flows will be received before and after this time, the average life serves as a good surrogate for comparing CMO performance with instruments of similar maturity. In addition to average life, an investor will also want to be aware of a CMO's principal payment window which estimates the first principal payment and final maturity for a given PSA level.

The CMO market has grown tremendously over the last several years offering investors new and attractive investment alternatives. Since the earliest structures developed in 1983, CMO's have evolved and now offer a wide range of structures that can provide more predictable cash flows than were previously available in the mortgage market. The comfort of AAA ratings along with very attractive relative yields make CMO's a suitable alternative for a broad range of investment objectives. **Only buy CMO's with long-term money, as the average life is not totally predictable.**

Some Investment Basics: A Re-Cap

Fixed-Income Securities: Call them notes, bonds, debentures, or bills. The concept is the same: a piece of paper that is a promise to repay a specific amount in the future. The issuer also pays the owner a specific interest rate (or "coupon rate") annually. Because that rate is fixed, the underlying value of the security can rise or fall as market interest rates fluctuate. Example: You pay $1,000 for a bond paying 12% interest ($120 a year), and maturing in ten years. If one year from now the prevailing rate on bonds is 14% ($140 a year), your bond might be only worth $855 — a price that would make the $120 annual interest equivalent to a 14% yield. Conversely, if market rates fall, your bond would increase in value.

Short-Term vs Long-Term: Economists constantly banter about "short-term" and "long-term" choices in fixed-income investing. Classically speaking, any security maturing in more than one year is a long-term security. But you also might hear these definitions: A maturity of one year or less is a very short-term, or "cash," investment. Securities maturing in one to five years are short-term (often called notes), those with five- to ten-year maturities are medium-term (called notes or bonds), and those maturing in ten years or more are long-term (known generally as bonds). Normally the longer the term, the higher the rate because you are taking more risk.

Bond Trading Made Simple

To many people, the bond market is an enigma, like the riddle of the Sphinx. One basic mystery: Why do people say the bond market is rallying when bond yields are falling? They say that because bond prices rise when yields fall. Here's why:

Bonds are IOU's that make fixed-interest payments until they mature. For example, a $1,000 30-year bond that pays 8% would pay $80 in interest every year for 30 years. Now, suppose demand for bonds is brisk and investors will buy new bonds that pay 7.5% interest. A bond with an 8% interest rate would look quite tempting to traders.

Since traders can't change a bond's interest payments, they bid up a bond's price. For example, if the 8% $1,000 bond's price rose to $1,060, its $80 annual interest payments would equal a 7.5% yield. Expecting interest rates to fall further, a trader would pay the premium for that 8% bond. Bond traders love to see yields fall. At current yields, a one-percentage point drop in rates would boost bond prices to about 9%. Rising interest rates reverse the process. When rates rise, traders bid bond prices down.

Finally, let's look at a sample bond portfolio. Figures #16-#19 provide an analysis of bond investments that follow prudent rules of portfolio composition. First, you will see a diversity of specific bond investments. Next, you will note a geographic diversity in distribution of investment dollars. You will also see a diversity of maturity dates (laddering effect) among the various bond investments. You will notice, however, that only AAA and AA bonds were chosen for this example — in other words, a conservative style was adopted.

In examining these figures, three concepts will be reinforced regarding your portfolio choices. They are diversity, duration, and dependability. As you examine the investment choices in subsequent chapters, you will apply these principles to those options, as well.

If you own bonds, ask a broker to prepare the following:

* The facts in the following figures have been obtained from outside sources, considered reliable, but no representation is made to their accuracy.

Examples were prepared for: Sample Portfolio.

Figure #16
PORTFOLIO HOLDINGS

Security Description	*	Maturity Value	Purchase Date	Purchase Price	S&P Rating	Maturity Date	Yield To Maturity
NEW YORK ST ENERGY RES OPT PUT 7/1/90 SUBJ TO AMT 5.75%	P	$5,000	07/84	$5,000	AAA	07/90	5.75%
NEW MEXICO EDL ASSISTANCE STUDENT LOAN SBJ TO AMT CAL 7.0%	P	$50,000	09/85	$49,000	AAA	09/90	6.90%
BERKS COUNTY PENNSYLVANIA MAND PUT 8.0%	P	$200,000	10/84	$200,000	AA	10/90	5.20%
LAFAYETTE LOUSIANNA UTILIT REV 8.25% PRE-FUNDED	R	$100,000	11/88	$100,000	AAA	11/92	6.19%
ALASKA ENERGY AUTH PWR REV 7.4%		$50,000	07/87	$51,999	AAA	07/93	6.35%
ALASKA STUDENT LOAN CORP SUBJ AMT CALL 7.40%		$50,000	07/87	$49,000	AAA	07/93	6.55%

* C - Callable, P - Putable, R - Pre-refunded

PORTFOLIO HOLDINGS

Security Description	*	Maturity Value	Purchase Date	Purchase Price	S&P Rating	Maturity Date	Yield To Maturity
AZLE TEXAS INDEP SCHOOL DST ESCROWED TO MATY 9.15%	C	$50,000	02/86	$50,000	AAA	02/94	6.58%
GREENVILLE SPARTANBURG SC SUBJ TO AMT 7.0		$50,000	07/87	$50,000	AAA	07/95	6.64%
IOWA STUDENT LOAN LIQ SUBJ TO AMT		$50,000	12/85	$51,500	AAA	12/95	6.98%
DALLAS COUNTY TEXAS 7.8% PUTABLE 7/10/96	P	$50,000	07/85	$48,750	AAA	07/96	6.99%
LOUSIANNA PUB FACS AUTH 7.20%	C	$25,000	09/85	$25,000	AAA	09/96	6.24%
FLORIDA HOUSING FINANCE AGENCY SUBJ TO AMT 7.45%	C	$50,000	12/88	$50,000	AAA	12/97	7.14%

C - Callable, P - Putable, R - Pre-refunded

102

PORTFOLIO HOLDINGS

Security Description	*	Maturity Value	Purchase Date	Purchase Price	S&P Rating	Maturity Date	Yield To Maturity
ILLINOIS HLTH FACLS AUTH 7.4%	C	$50,000	08/87	$50,000	AAA	08/98	6.83%
HAWAII ST DEPT BUD & FIN OPT PUT 7.375%	P	$100,000	09/88	$100,000	AAA	09/98	7.15%
LOWER COLORADO RIVER AUTH TEXAS REV 7.0	P	$50,000	01/87	$49,000	AAA	01/99	7.01%
NORTH DAKOTA ST STU-DENT LOAN 7.50%	C	$50,000	07/88	$51,000	AAA	07/99	7.31%
TYLER TEX HLTH FACS DV 8.0%	C	$50,000	11/88	$50,000	AA	11/00	7.48%
PORTFOLIO VALUE AT MATURITY		$1,030,000		TOTAL PURCHASE PRICE $1,030,249			

C - Callable, P - Putable, R - Pre-refunded

Figure #17

MATURITY DISTRIBUTION

Year	Principal Value At Maturity	% of Total Portfolio
1990	$255,000	24.76%
1991		
1992	$100,000	9.71%
1993	$100,000	9.71%
1994	$50,000	4.85%
1995	$100,000	9.71%
1996	$75,000	7.28%
1997	$50,000	4.85%
1998	$150,000	14.56%
1999	$100,000	9.71%
2000	$50,000	4.85%
2001		
2002		
2003		
2004		
2005		
2006		
2007		
2008		
2009		
2010		
2011		
2012		
2013		
2014		
2015		
2016		
2017		
2018		
2019		

Total Principal at Maturity: $ 1,030,000

Maturity Distribution
Prepared for: Sample Portfolio

Thousands

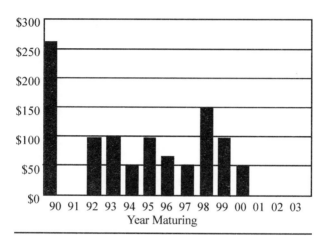

Year Maturing

Figure #18

RATING DISTRIBUTION

S&P Rating	Principal	%of Total Portfolio
AAA	$780,000	75.73%
AA	$250,000	24.27%
A		
BBB		
BB		
B		
CCC		
CC		
C		
DDD		
DD		
D		
NR		

Total Principal at Maturity: $1,030,000

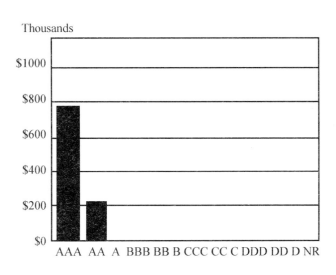

Winning The Money Game Made Easy

**Rating Distribution
Prepared for: Sample Portfolio**

Thousands

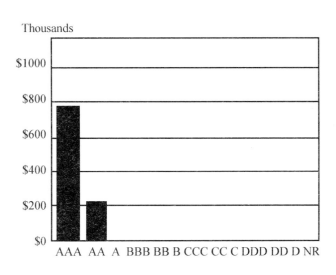

106

Figure #19
GEOGRAPHIC DISTRIBUTION

State Issued	Issuer	Principal	% of Total Portfolio
AK	ALASKA ENERGY AUTH PWR REV	$50,000	4.9%
	ALASKA STUDENT LOAN CORP	$50,000	4.9%
	TOTAL:	$100,000	9.6%
CO	LOWER COLORADO RIVER AUTH	$50,000	4.9%
	TOTAL	$50,000	4.8%
FL	FLORIDA HOUSING FINANCE	$50,000	4.9%
	TOTAL:	$50,000	4.8%
HI	HAWAII ST DEPT BUD & FIN	$100,000	9.7%
	TOTAL:	$100,000	9.7%
IA	IOWA STUDENT LOAN LIQ SUBJ	$50,000	4.9%
	TOTAL:	$50,000	4.8%
IL	ILLINOIS HLTH FACLS AUTH	$50,000	4.9%

GEOGRAPHIC DISTRIBUTION

State Issued	Issuer	Principal	% of Total Portfolio
TOTAL		$50,000	4.8%
LA	LAFAYETTE LOUSIANNA UTILIT LOUSIANNA PUB FACS AUTH TOTAL:	$100,000 $ 25,000 $125,000	9.7% 2.4% 12.1%
ND	NORTH DAKOTA ST STUDENT LN TOTAL:	$50,000 $50,000	4.9% 4.8%
NM	NEW MEXICO EDL ASSISTANCE TOTAL:	$50,000 $50,000	4.9% 4.8%
NY	NEW YORK ST ENERGY RES OPT	$5,000	0.5%

GEOGRAPHIC DISTRIBUTION

State Issued	Issuer	Principal	% of Total Portfolio
TOTAL		$5,000	0.4%
PA	BERKS COUNTY PENSYLVANIA TOTAL:	$200,000 $200,000	19.4% 19.4%
SC	GREENVILLE SPARTANBURG SC TOTAL:	$50,000 $50,000	4.9% 4.8%
TX	DALLAS COUNTY TEXAS AZLE TEXAS INDEP SCHOOL DST TYLER TEX HLTH FACS DV TOTAL:	$50,000 $50,000 $50,000 $150,000	4.9% 4.9% 4.9% 14.4%

Total Principal at Maturity: $ 1,030,000

Chapter 4

Stocks

"You can't steal second base without taking your foot off first."

Unknown

A Brief History

In 1653, a 12-foot high stockade was erected across lower Manhattan (then called New Amsterdam), to protect the Dutch settlers from attacks by the British and Indians. In spite of the "wall", the British captured the area and re-named it New York. Surveyors laid out Wall Street where the stockade had been.

Many years later in 1792, twenty-four prominent brokers and merchants met under a buttonwood tree on Wall Street and started buying pieces of each other's companies.

The birth of the New York Stock Exchange occurred when these brokers and merchants signed the "Buttonwood Agreement". Those who signed agreed to trade securities on a common commission basis.

The year 1817 brought the trading indoors when they rented a meeting room at 40 Wall Street and formally established the New York Stock Exchange.

The New York Stock Exchange (NYSE) now lists and trades approximately 2,000 stocks, almost 1,000 corporate bonds, nearly 400 convertible bonds and over 200 convertible preferred stocks. A multi-million dollar, space-age order execution computer accepts orders from around the world with equal ease in this public, two-way auction market. The Dutch businessmen of long ago would be as shocked to see the mechanics of today's market as modern folks would be to see a stockade in Manhattan. Technology!

How Stock Originates

Companies in need of funding for start-up or growth have two primary choices for acquiring needed dollars: debt capital and equity capital. Money acquired through borrowing or bond issuance is called debt capital. Funds

111

acquired in this way must be paid back to the bank or investors.

In the case of equity capital, new investors exchange their capital (money) for equity (ownership) in the company. In other words, these investors become part-owners of the company on a pro-rated basis.

The need for capital sets in motion the process that results in stock formation and sale. Without outside capital, a company's growth potential is limited because the money to finance new facilities, research, or new product development must come largely from retained earnings or loans.

Once the decision has been made to acquire funds through the sale of equity, the next step in the process is the formation of a corporation. To do this, a company must file articles of incorporation with the secretary of state's office.

Stocks are issued only by a publicly owned corporation, a form of legal organization adopted by most large, modern businesses. Smaller enterprises are frequently organized as privately held corporations, partnerships, individual proprietorships, or limited partnerships. However, when a business starts to grow enough to require outside funding or capital, a corporation form of organization becomes essential.

Now that the corporation has been formed, it must appoint its first board of directors to oversee management of the company. (Later on, the board of directors will be elected by the shareholders.) These directors will determine how many shares of stock will be created by dividing the total dollar amount of desired capital into equal "pieces of ownership." If, for example, a company needed to raise $1,000,000 in equity capital, it could issue 100,000 shares at $10.00 each or 50,000 shares at $20.00 each, etc.

After the initial (par) value and number of shares of

stock have been determined, the company's investment banker offers the stock for sale to the public. Finally, the company will issue the shares to the purchasers in the form of stock certificates.

The companies' profits can be retained for future needs or disbursed among the shareholders. These payments can take the form of cash dividends which are taxable income. A company can also issue shares of stock as dividends that are not taxable. I will discuss dividends in more detail later in the chapter.

Stock Terminology

In order to understand the role of stock in your personal investment portfolio, you must understand the terms in which it is discussed. I will introduce some of them here to get you started, and will introduce others during the appropriate discussion.

Stock is often labeled with a term that describes its current status in a company. A corporation may choose not to sell all of the shares of stock it has created. The status of shares of stock are, therefore, described in the following terms:

1. *Authorized* — describes all shares that have been authorized by the board of directors, approved for current and future distribution (sale).
2. *Issued* — refers to the number of shares that have been sold or are outstanding.
3. *Treasury* — refers to shares that are not issued, those that have never been sold, or those that the company has repurchased, that are held by the corporation for the following reasons:
    A. for stock option plans, employee purchase plans, bonus plans
    B. to buy other companies via a "stock swap"

113

C. to "shore up the stock value; the fewer the outstanding shares, the more they are worth.

The following terms refer to particular types of stock. **Common and Preferred Stock.** Both types of stock represent fractional ownership of a company. Investors or stockholders give capital to a company in exchange for the chance to share in the potential growth and profit of that company. The primary difference between common and preferred stock is that common stock is growth oriented, and preferred stock is income oriented. Common stocks represent the highest volume of stocks traded on the New York Stock Exchange. Most individuals will own common stock, as opposed to preferred stock.

Blue-Chip Stocks. This term derives from the high value of blue poker chips. Ironically, investing in these stocks is supposed to be anything but a poker game. While you will not find a specific financial definition of a blue-chip company, this designation generally refers to those companies who are the giants of their particular industries.

Blue-chips are represented in the Dow Jones 30 industrial stocks and Standard & Poor's 500 Index. They have long and mostly profitable histories. There is little risk that they will disappear next year or in the near future, although they can be buffeted by the economic cycle like any other company. Cash dividend payments from these companies are usually substantial and dependable.

Large Capitalization Stocks. This term also denotes a major company, although not necessarily of the caliber of a blue-chip. The number of outstanding shares multiplied by the share price is equal to the market capitalization. That is, theoretically, what the market thinks the company is worth at any given time. For example, at $49.00 per share with 571,000,000 shares outstanding,

114

Wall Street estimated that IBM Corporation was worth $27.9 billion dollars in 1993. That was the value of all its property, employees, and technology. In 1995 at $80.00 per share x 571,000,000 shares outstanding, the capitalization is $45.6 billion dollars. Much more than originally thought.

When a company's worth is calculated by this formula to be worth one billion dollars or more, its stock is large capitalization. Companies with a value of at least half a billion, but under a billion dollars are middle capitalization; companies valued under half a billion dollars are small capitalization, according to most Wall Street Wizards.

Large capitalization companies are generally household words, like Proctor and Gamble, General Motors, General Electric, AT & T, and IBM, etc.

Secondary Stocks. This is a generic term embracing the smallest companies on the New York Stock Exchange and most companies on both the American Stock Exchange and the National Association of Securities Dealers Automated Quotations system (NASDAQ). NASDAQ is the principal over-the-counter market trading, approximately 15,000 stocks. These are generally small capitalization stocks.

Growth Stocks. Traditionally, growth stock is stock issued by a company that retains most of its earnings rather than paying a large share to stockholders. Because smaller companies generally do not pay dividends, their stocks are often labeled growth. A more accurate definition would be the stock of a company whose earnings are expected to grow faster than the economy of the Standard & Poor's 500 average. This definition embraces many large companies as well as small ones. Note that the terms *growth stock* and *secondary stock* are not necessarily synonymous.

Convertible Preferred Stock. Convertible preferred

stock has many of the same characteristics of the convertible bonds I discussed in the previous chapter. The major difference, of course, is that stock is equity rather than debt. Convertible stocks do not have maturity dates, but are subject to redemption.

Some Basics in the Marketing of Stock

Investment bankers usually underwrite a new issue of stock. The bankers buy it from the issuing company and sell it to investors at a mark-up. When you purchase a stock, you will receive a stock certificate from the company's transfer agent. The transfer agent keeps track of all shareholders in that company. Your stock certificate will contain brief information about the company and will outline its obligation to you as a stockholder. You may choose to have a bank or brokerage firm hold your shares; they will be insured against loss, so you will not run the risk of misplacing them. If you choose to have personal possession of your certificate, do not lose it unless you welcome the unnecessary ordeal and cost to track it down and replace it.

Once the public owns the stock, trading begins in the secondary market. The New York Stock Exchange (NYSE) is the world's largest secondary market. When you buy an individual stock, you must pay for it within three business or five calendar days. When you sell it, you will receive payment within the same three to five day time frame.

While the investment banker and company set the initial price, the prices in the open market will reflect the investors' perceptions of the company's profits. Many factors can influence the perception of a stock's value: in other words, the price. They can range from events affecting only one company to events impacting an entire industry. The United States economy, the global economic outlook and occasionally, political and emotional factors such as international tensions, affect stock prices.

You cannot adequately analyze a company without considering the context in which it operates. Is the industry seriously vulnerable to foreign competition? How dependent are its products on certain commodities? Are the raw materials it requires for production subject to sudden price increases or shortages? Will it be adversely affected by changes in foreign exchange rates? These are some of the questions you might ask in analyzing the value of a company's stock.

Stock prices are also affected by changing interest rates. Higher interest rates may attract investor funds to debt securities when the return on interest bearing securities exceeds the return on stocks expected to provide current income. Thus, preferred stocks are especially sensitive to interest rate changes because they are bought primarily for income purposes. General prosperity here in the United States or in foreign countries can affect a company's sales and, therefore, the price of its stock.

Recent sales, profits, and the outlook for future profits usually exert the greatest influence on stock prices at the company level and are a key measure of company success. Projections for a company's future success must take in to account a vast number of factors including the following:

- *the uniqueness of its product*
- *its competitive position and potential*
- *sales and industry trends*
- *management practices*

In addition, investors should know the answers to such questions as:

- *How inventive is the company?*
- *Does it have a good image in the public eye?*
- *Is its failure threatened with hostile regulation or legislation?*

Investors often bid up the price of stock for a company attractive to takeover bids. A company's ability to absorb another company can also enhance its market value. The rules of supply and demand that affect the price of goods and services apply to the world of stocks, as well. How much interest is there at the moment among investors to buy and sell the stock?

Your Securities and the New York Stock Exchange

Many investors are attracted to the NYSE for a number of reasons. It lists some of the world's largest and best-managed corporations. It is the largest secondary stock market in the world, trading over 3,500 stocks and bonds. With its powerful, space-age computer system, the Exchange can handle orders from around the world and around the block, equally. The NYSE can track large buys and sells with phenomenal speed and efficiency. While the "Hollywood" picture of trading is often full of waving arms, frantic shouts, and papers flying through the air, the NYSE is actually an orderly organization.

The two-way market of the NYSE is pure, unexpurgated capitalism — free enterprise at its finest. Since the shares traded on the floor are already issued, there must be a buyer for every seller. For every transaction, someone believes he is selling for all the right reasons, and someone else believes he is buying for the right reasons. That is probably the best example of supply and demand theory there is. That is why prices go up and down.

Many investors choose to do business with NYSE member firms where they can expect to receive the same efficient service as they receive directly on the trading floor. Whether on the trading floor or in the office, member firms strive to provide efficient order execution, meeting their customers needs by obtaining the best available prices at the lowest possible cost with all due speed. Among such firms are Merrill Lynch, Dean Witter, Reynolds, and Stifel Nicolaus among others.

Even after being in the business for eighteen years, I am still amazed at the lightening speed and accuracy with which transactions can be made. One Friday afternoon, I traded 4,000 shares of a $150.00 stock from my office in Beloit, Wisconsin for a client who was sitting across the desk from me. Within two minutes of his decision to sell that stock at specified price, we had the order execution back from New York — on paper! Both this gentleman, who had been active in the stock market for about fifty years, and I, were astounded by the advancements in technology that made such a move possible. Tens of thousands of dollars changed hands from New York to Beloit and back in a two-minute time period!

Securities Industry Regulation

Since the early 1930's, the Securities and Exchange Commission, a federal agency, has closely regulated issuance, sales, and trading of securities. Laws generally prescribe what information publicly held corporations must disclose to stockholders, the way brokerage firms must conduct business and the manner in which securities trading is to be conducted.

Beyond this, the securities industry also has its own detailed code of self-regulation that sets standards for doing business with the public and lays down rules for maintaining fair and orderly securities markets.

As I stated earlier, though a few tainted traders have captured notoriety in recent years, the overwhelming majority of folks in the industry are honest, industrious, and dedicated to making money for their customers. In fact, the NYSE is so rigid in its review of members, that the Securities and Exchange Commission generally does not impose any regulations above and beyond what it imposes on itself.

Surveys have shown that public investors generally rank surveillance of trading and regulatory monitoring of member firms' activities among the most importance on insuring the integrity of its members and transactions.

What You Should Know About Owning Stock

At last count, over fifty-eight million people in the United States owned stock in publicly traded companies — more than one out of six! And here's another "believe it or not" — the NYSE profile of the typical shareowner is a 44 1/2-year old female member of a household with a $46,300 income and an investment portfolio worth approximately $21,850.

Figure #20 illustrates the performance of a variety of investment vehicles over a period of six decades. Notice the position of stock in relation to other types of investments.

Depending on your age, investing style, and stage in life, stock may make up between 15% and 80% of your investment portfolio with the highest percentage being invested in your middle years.

The following graph shows performance of investment categories since 1925, and can help you match your time horizons to appropriate investment categories.

Figure #20
Investment History of $1 Invested in 1925

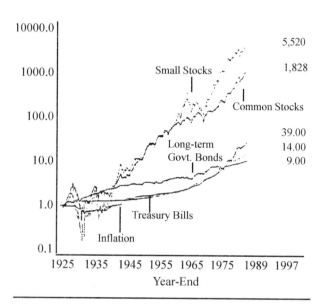

The sections that follow will help you understand what your rights and privileges are as a shareholder, what returns you can expect on your stock investment, how to select stock and build a stock plan, and how to read the stock pages.

Owning Common Stock

Common stock, representing fractional shares of ownership in a corporation, give shareholders certain rights.

The right to dividends. When a company makes profits, the board of directors may vote to share the profits by distributing dividends among common stockholders, in proportion to the shares they own. They are not required by law to pay them.

The right to share in growth or capital appreciation. There is no guarantee that the value of your stock will increase, but you can reasonably expect share prices will rise if the company does well. Conversely, if the company does poorly, it would most likely be reflected by a drop in the value of the shares.

The right to transfer. If you sell or give away your stock, the change in ownership is recorded on the books of the corporation through a well-established transfer procedure.

The right to be kept informed. Under law and the rules applying to New York Stock Exchange-listed companies, shareholders are entitled to annual and interim reports. Also, the company is obligated to publicly disclose, usually through the media, most corporate developments that might have a major effect on shareholders or the value of their stock. Companies mail regular reports to shareholders, but you should also watch the financial media for other news affecting a company whose stock you own.

The right to a voice in corporate decisions. Shareholders have voting rights at shareholder meetings either in person or by proxy. Under federal and NYSE rules, all recorded shareholders must be given proxy statements explaining issues scheduled for voting at the meeting. The statement must also provide other important company information. Holders of common stock also are subject to certain limitations. Common stock is junior in standing to corporate debt (bonds) and to preferred stock. In this case, Junior refers to bondholders' claims to interest payments or preferred stockholders' claims to dividends taking priority over any dividend stock payment. If the company is liquidated, bondholders, and preferred stockholders must be paid before any funds can be distributed to common stockholders.

Bradley Gummow

Preferred Stocks

Because preferred stockholders have priority in receiving income and claims on any company assets, many investors include some preferred stocks in their holdings. The benefits of investing in preferreds often are similar to those of bonds.

Preferred stockholders have an ownership interest in the company's net worth — what is left after all debts (liabilities), operating costs and taxes are subtracted from total assets. Preferred stock is subordinate, (or junior) to the company's debts to bondholders but senior to common stock. Preferred dividends usually are paid at a fixed rate.

Although the rate is fixed, dividends may be decreased or omitted at the discretion of the company's directors, unlike mandatory bond interest payments. However, preferred stock dividends would normally be paid before dividends on common stock. Most preferred stock dividends are cumulative — meaning omitted dividends are accumulated and must be paid in total before common stock dividends can be paid.

Most preferred stocks do not have voting rights. However, some corporations may offer preferred stockholders that additional protection of voting rights, but only subject to certain conditions such as after a specified number of dividends have been paid.

You might select preferred stocks for a higher return. Preferred stocks often earn a better return than savings accounts and dividends on common stocks, depending on a company's financial success. Greater safety of principal is a common attraction of high quality preferreds. The provision of many preferreds allow reasonable certainty that the stated annual dividend rate will be paid, assuming enough is earned by the company. In case of bankruptcy or liquidation, preferred has priority of dist-

123

ribution of assets over common.

Preferred stocks offer relative safety of income, but their prices usually have more modest growth potential than common stocks, a trade-off accepted of investors seeking assured income.

Dividends, Stock Dividends, and Splits

Most people expect their largest reward from common stocks to come from price appreciation, netting a gain when the stock is sold. Dividend income is also an important consideration.

Companies issuing stock, however, usually are not legally required to pay dividends on common stock. Dividends on preferred stock, while mandatory under the terms of issuance, do not necessarily have to be paid at the specified time. While they may be deferred if the directors believe it necessary, they eventually must be paid. Until an unpaid preferred dividend is paid, dividends cannot be paid on common stock.

Because developing companies may use most of their earnings to finance future growth, they may pay very small cash dividends or none at all. With the exception of preferred stock, there is no rule set on how much of its earnings a company distributes as dividends or how often. The directors set the payout rate and time and who may decide on other uses of company earnings.

A company may want to give present or potential shareholders an incentive while still conserving cash by occasionally paying a dividend in shares of stock — stock dividends — rather than cash. These additional shares have a value closely related to those already outstanding. However, the market price of outstanding shares sometimes declines after a stock dividend, reflecting the greater number of shares that will participate in a payout of the company's earnings.

A stock split is another type of distribution of additional shares. In a split, the outstanding shares are divided into a larger number of shares. A 3-for-1 split of 1 million outstanding shares results in a new total of 3 million outstanding shares. A stockholder's potential equity in the company remains the same.

In theory, per share price after the split should be one-third of the pre-split price and, since the number the of shares triples, there should be no change in the value of a shareowner's total holdings. For example, if you hold 100 shares of a $60.00 stock worth $6,000 after a 3-for-1 split, your post split holding would be 300 shares at $20.00 per share, still worth $6,000.

Rights and Warrants

A company trying to raise funds by issuing additional securities may give stockholders first chance or "right" to buy the new securities in proportion to their current holdings. After the corporation announces a "rights" offer, stock owners receive "rights" certificates. Because "right" represents the value between the market price and the price of the new securities, they have a value around which a market will develop. Trading in this "rights" market can be fairly active, since the right must be exercised in a short time.

Warrants are also certificates to purchase stock. Warrants are generally offered as a part of a package when a corporation sells shares to raise new capital. To give investors more incentive to buy the new shares, warrants will sometimes be attached. Each new share purchased gives the buyer a specific number of warrants, allowing the purchase of a specified number of shares, either at a set date or any time in the future.

Warrants, however, have a number of features distin-

guishing them from "rights". Warrants are long-term instruments that can be exercised as much as five to ten
years later. In addition, when they are issued, warrants
are priced above the prevailing market price for the security — just the opposite of "rights". Rights and warrants,
which apply to newly issued securities, should not be confused with a split of existing shares or a stock dividend
paid to existing shareholders in the lieu of a cash dividend.

Selecting a Stock for Your Portfolio

It is my considered opinion — after learning the hard
way — that it is important to adopt a long-term approach
to the stock market. Learn to forego the need for immediate gratification.

Lack of patience is the largest impediment to success
in the market. A former colleague of mine used to say,
"Stocks go up and down. Thank goodness they mainly
go up." In other words, look at the big picture. In 42 of
the last 50 years (as of this writing), stocks (as a group),
have advanced.

I started in this business at the advanced and mature
age of twenty-four. Naturally I knew everything necessary to beat the market. Within a relatively short period
of time, I came to a startling revelation: You have to play
by the rules.

The rules are this:
1. *Be humble or the market will teach you to be.*
2. *Exercise patience at appropriate times.*
3. *Cut losses: Don't fall in love with a stock.*
4. *Buy quality companies: market leaders, companies that dominate their business.*
5. *Gray is the color of the market — **not** black or
   white. In other words, be flexible. Unsettling news
   can disrupt the best-laid plans. "Hot tips" or*

126

*enticements are also a pitfall to avoid. By the time a
"hot tip" reaches you or me, it has probably
become "cold".*

Stock Selection

When choosing an analyst, you should be sure that
their premise of stock selection agrees with your principles. Fundamental and Technical Analysis are the two
approaches I discuss here.

Fundamental Analysis

Fundamental Analysis is an approach based on
mathematic formulas, and a corporation's balance sheet
and income statement, and strengths and weaknesses
through economic and industry trends. The following selections are criteria of the highly successful Heartland
Value Funds of Milwaukee, Wisconsin.

Earnings Growth. The company must demonstrate
sustained earnings growth. Earnings from continuing operations should have doubled in the last ten years. The
quality of earnings, based on conservative accounting
practices, is an important factor. Confidence in earnings
predictability also is important.

Dividend Stability. The dividend must not have been
cut more than once in the last ten years. Dividends that
are consistent and which increase regularly are given
multiple preference in weighting. This demonstrates
management's ability to handle cash flow and earnings
for the benefit of shareholders.

Low Price/Earnings Ratio. The stock's price to earnings ratio should be less than the market's general multiple. This provides the opportunity for expansion. A low
multiple prevents the purchase of a stock that could have
considerable risk if earnings contract.

127

Discount to Book Value. The stock should be selling below its tangible book value per share. (Tangible book value is equal to total assets minus all liabilities and good will.) Changes in earnings and price/earnings ratios can be sudden and violent. However, changes in book value are more gradual. Book value represents an intrinsic value which is more representative of the worth of the company than its daily price quotation.

High Liquidity. The company's current assets less current liabilities and long-term debt, per share, should be higher in relation to the price of the stock.

Financial Soundness. The long-term debt should be less than 40% of the total capitalization. During difficult periods, a company's cash flow should be directed to investments in operations rather than interest expense. A highly leveraged balance sheet can be become a hindrance to performance and financial soundness.

Quality Management. The company should be run by capable and honest management with a history of being reasonable and fair to all shareholders.

Shareholder Base. Ownership of the stock should be weighted towards insiders and away from institutions. Management and directors should have their personal wealth invested in the company and its performance. Companies shrinking their capitalization through the repurchase of stock and the reduction of debt are preferred.

Hidden Assets. Assets that are not on the balance sheet are considered additional value. Hidden assets as a LIFO (Last In, First Out Accounting Method), reserve, high appraised value, understated natural resource assets, or an over-funded pension plan can significantly add to shareholder net worth.

High Cash Flow. Cash flow per share should be considerably higher than earnings per share. It has been demonstrated that strong cash flow allows a company to generate greater wealth over the long-term. Debt does not need to be added as quickly, if at all, for expansion or reinvestment. After all capital expenditures and dividends, a high discretionary cash flow is very attractive.

Chart Pattern. Technical analysis should indicate that a stock is presently attractive for investing without undue speculation. Chart patterns show the history of a stock's price and the volume of its trading at various levels. We typically seek "bases" in a stock's patterns on the belief that speculators will not own the stock or be interested in it at that moment. Reading the chart of a stock is often an art, but in today's market it is a necessary skill to complement our fundamental analysis.

When using fundamental analysis, an analyst may also become familiar with a company's products, customers, and suppliers.

An analyst may also look for something new to create interest in the stock — new management, new products, etc. Remember, the stock market is, in my opinion, the best example of the Law of Supply and Demand. Create a demand, and the existing supply becomes highly desirable.

Technical Analysis

Technical analysis bases predictions on price trends and their relationship to present and prior trends. The use of charts of price movement are what a true technician cares about, not the name or product of a company. The things they look for are:

Break-Outs. A stock moving out (up) of a base pattern. The premise being that stocks setting new highs, tend to set more new highs.

Volume. A stock going up on increased volume generally indicates greater interest in the stock.

Resistance Levels. Where a price may run into a ceiling of resistance.

Support Levels. As the name implies, a level where buying interest may develop to the point providing a "turn around" point.

Relative Strength. How well the stock price is behaving relative to all other stock prices.

Reviewing Your Stock Portfolio

Your portfolio may need to be re-balanced from time to time. Every ninety days, (each quarter), I would encourage you to closely examine your stock portfolio. Figures #21-#25 on pages 102-104, may serve as a guideline for a step by step review of your portfolio.

Review your gains and losses (Figure #21). This can help keep small losses from becoming too large. Also, when examining the gains, remember that bulls and bears make money, and hogs get slaughtered. Don't be a hog.

Pay close attention to income from your stocks (Figure #22). Note how yield levels change with price movement. Is the income from your stock portfolio at the level you want it to be?

Figure #23 shows an excellent method of measuring the "value" of your holdings. Value is measured in P/E ratios. Price-Earnings ratios are a very basic method of determining a stock's value in relation to the earnings of the company. Price-Earnings is the price of the stock divided into the earnings per share; i.e., a $10 stock with $1 per share in earnings represents a P/E of 10.

Safety should be a serious consideration in your stock portfolio. You must be comfortable with the amount of risk in each of your equity investments (Figure #24).

Figure #25, Diversifying by Industry, is akin to not keeping all your eggs in one basket. I normally suggest 3-5 different industries. Looking at the percentage each investment holds in your portfolio will help maintain diversification. Ask your broker to prepare the following for your portfolio:

130

Figure #21
Sample Portfolio: Gains and Losses

SHARES HELD	COMPANY NAME	PURCHASE PRICE	CURRENT PRICE	VALUE OF HOLDINGS	GAIN OR LOSS	% GAIN OR LOSS
100	AMR Corporation	$54.50	$58.13	$ 5,813	$ 362.50	6.7
400	BankAmerica	$25.13	$36.38	$14,550	$4,498.00	44.8
300	BellSouth Corporation	$52.38	$53.75	$16,125	$ 411.00	2.6
200	Boeing	$32.38	$48.13	$ 9,625	$3,148.99	48.6
100	Common Wealth Edison	$34.13	$39.50	$ 3,950	$ 536.99	15.7
200	Gillette	$38.94	$76.13	$15,225	$7,437.00	95.5
200	TRW Incorporated	$42.50	$40.38	$ 8,075	$ (425.00)	-5.0
100	Union Carbide	$23.44	$17.00	$ 1,700	$ (644.00)	-27.5
1600 Total/Averages				$75,063	$15,325.48	25.7

Figure #22
Sample Portfolio: Income Report

SHARES HELD	COMPANY NAME	CURRENT PRICE	VALUE OF HOLDINGS	CURRENT DIVIDEND	ESTIMATED INCOME	CURRENT YIELD
100	AMR Corporation	$53.13	$ 5,813	$0.00	$ 0.00	0.0
400	BankAmerica	$36.38	$14,550	$1.20	$ 480.00	3.3
300	BellSouth Corporation	$53.75	$16,125	$2.84	$ 852.00	5.3
200	Boeing	$48.13	$ 9,622	$1.10	$ 220.00	2.3
100	Common Wealth Edison	$39.50	$ 3,950	$3.00	$ 300.00	7.6
200	Gillette	$76.13	$15,225	$1.24	$ 248.00	1.6
200	TRW Incorporated	$40.38	$ 8,075	$1.80	$ 360.00	4.5
100	Union Carbide	$17.00	$ 1,700	$1.00	$ 100.00	5.9
1600 Total/Averages			$75,063	$1.61	$2,560.00	3.4

Figure #23
Sample Portfolio: Valuation Report

COMPANY NAME	RECENT PRICE	CURRENT P-E	CURRENT YIELD	PRICE/ BOOK VALUE	EST % CHG EPS FY	PRJ EPS* GROWTH
AMR Corporation	$58.13	NA	0.0	0.96	NA	12.0
BankAmerica	$36.38	8.7	3.3	1.59	14.6	NA
BellSouth Corporation	$53.75	15.6	5.3	1.98	12.1	7.5
Boeing	$48.13	10.9	2.3	2.38	31.5	26.0
Common Wealth Edison	$39.50	12.5	7.6	1.21	NA	4.0
Gillette	$76.13	20.6	1.6	105.73	21.9	17.5
TRW Incorporated	$40.38	11.4	4.5	1.30	13.6	10.0
Union Carbide	$17.00	11.0	5.9	1.01	-37.8	-12.5
Totals/Averages	$51.52	13.8	3.4	22.78	16.7	12.9

*Earnings per share on an annual basis.

Figure #24
Sample Portfolio: Diversification by Safety

SAFETY RANK*	BETA*	COMPANY NAME	SHARES HELD	CURRENT PRICE	VALUE OF HOLDINGS	PCT OF PORTFOLIO
1	0.90	BellSouth Corporation	300	$53.75	$ 16,125	21.5
1	0.95	Boeing	200	$48.13	$ 9,625	12.8
1	**0.92 Group Totals/Averages**		**500**		**$ 25,750**	**34.3**
2	1.05	TRW incorporated	200	$40.38	$ 8,075	10.8
2	**1.05 Group Totals/Averages**		**200**		**$ 8,075**	**10.8**
3	1.35	AMR Corporation	100	$58.13	$ 5,813	7.7
3	1.25	Union Carbide	100	$17.00	$ 1,700	2.3
3	1.10	Bank America	400	$36.38	$ 14,550	19.4
3	1.20	Gillette	200	$76.13	$ 15,225	20.3
3	0.80	Common Wealth Edison	100	$39.50	$ 3,950	5.3
3	**1.15 Group Totals/Averages**		**900**		**$ 41,238**	**54.9**

*Safety rated by Value Line. On a scale of 1-5 in this example, 1 is the safest. **Beta is the scale of volatility. The volatility of the stock market is ranked 1. A stock with a Beta of 1.2 is 20% more volatile than the market as a whole.

Figure #25
Sample Portfolio: Diversification

Company Name	Shares Held	Current Price	Value of Holdings	% of Portfolio
Union Carbide	100	$17.00	$ 1,700	2.3
Group Totals/Avgs	**100**		**$ 1,700**	**2.3**
Gillette	200	$76.13	$ 15,225	20.3
Group Totals/Avgs	**200**		**$ 15,225**	**20.3**
Boeing	200	$48.13	$ 9,625	12.8
Group Totals/Avgs	**200**		**$ 9,625**	**12.8**
AMR Corporation	100	$58.13	$ 5,813	7.7
Group Totals/Avgs	**100**		**$ 5,813**	**7.7**
BellSouth Corporation	300	$53.75	$16,125	21.5
Group Totals/Avgs	**300**		**$16,125**	**21.5**
Common Wealth Edition	100	$39.50	$ 3,950	5.3
Group Totals/Avgs	**100**		**$ 3,950**	**5.3**
BankAmerica	400	$36.38	$14,550	19.4
Group Totals/Avg	**400**		**$14,550**	**19.4**
TRW Incorporated	200	$40.38	8075.00	10.8
Group Totals/Avgs	**200**		**8075.00**	**10.8**
Totals/Averages	**1600**		**75,062.50**	**100.0**

How to Read the Stock Page

Now that you have discovered what is important in stock selection for your portfolio — types of stock, privileges of ownership, analysis — you will want to watch the performance of your securities in the stock pages. Figure #26 is an example of a stock quote from the Wall Street Journal. It is American Telephone and Telegraph's performance on the previous trading day.

Figure #26
How to Read the Stock Page

---

52 weeks					Yld			Vol	Net	
Hi	Lo	Stock	Sym	Div	%	PE	100's	Hi	Lo	Close
Chg										
513/4	365/8	AmT&T	T	1.32	2.5	20	x18091	523/4	511/2	523/4
+1/2										

The Wall Street Journal, Monday, December 28, 1992.

---

51 3/4 is the highest price the stock has traded at, in the 52 weeks prior to today. Note the new high.

+1 1/2 is the change for the day.

36 5/8 is the lowest price the stock had traded at in the 52 weeks prior to today.

AmT&T is the Wall Street Journal's own abbreviation.

T is the quote symbol used by brokers and the exchanges.

1.32 is the annual dividend, $0.33 in each of the four quarters.

2.5% is the current yield: dividend divided into the share price. Example: $1.32 divided by 52 3/4.

20 is the price-earning ratio. The current earnings per share, divided into the current price.

136

18091 is the volume on this day. 1,809,100 shares traded hands.

52 3/4 was the high for the day.

51 1/2 was the low for the day.

52 3/4 is the closing price for the day.

You will notice that stocks trade in 1/8 of a point. It seems archaic, nonetheless, we need to understand it. 1 point equals $1.00, therefore:

1/8 = .125	5/8 = .625
1/4 = .25	3/4 = .75
3/8 = .375	7/8 = .875
1/2 = .50	1 = 1.00

(Some information contained in this chapter is provided by the New York Stock Exchange, an excellent source for the investing public.)

Chapter 5

Mutual Funds

"Compounding may very well be the eighth wonder of the world."

J. Paul Morgan

Bradley Gummow

What is a Mutual Fund?

Mutual funds were first introduced in the United States over fifty years ago. With over 8,500 mutual funds currently available, mutual fund ownership has virtually exploded in the last fifteen years. Today, over thirty million people are shareholders in mutual funds. Figure #27 - #31 provide information on the extent of participation and typical profiles of today's investors. Figures #27 and #28 illustrate the increase in participation over a twelve-year period by the percentage and number of households. Figures #29-#31 profile investors by such factors as gender, education, marital status, experience, and income.

What is a mutual fund? It is a company that combines the investment funds of many people whose investment goals are similar, and in turn, invests the money in a wide variety of securities. The selection, monitoring, and sale of individual securities is under the continuous supervision of professional investment managers.

Mutual funds seek to do for the individual what he might do for himself if he had the time, the inclination, the experience, and sufficient resources to spread his investments among many businesses and industries. Buying into mutual funds can be a sort of "one-stop-shopping" experience, allowing an investor to purchase diversification of assets, high-volume buying power, market experience, and regular, professional management — all under one roof.

The sum of the various investments is known as the company's portfolio. Common and preferred stocks and corporate and municipal bonds are among the portfolio securities in which a company may invest. Thus, the shares a mutual fund investor owns may represent an indirect interest in the investment results of from fifty to over a hundred securities.

139

The mutual fund market offers a wide range of investment objectives, management policies, and degrees of risk and profit. For example, some funds place primary emphasis on capital growth with current income being only a secondary consideration. Others stress income, preservation of capital, or a balance between growth and income to achieve their stated goals.

Mutual funds are technically known as open-end investment companies because they stand ready at any time to redeem outstanding shares when presented by the investor. Therefore, the number of shares is not fixed; the outstanding total will vary as new shares are sold to investors and other shares are redeemed by the company.

A mutual fund trades shares at net asset value. The result of the total value of a company's investments, divided by the number of shares owned by that fund is the net asset value. This dollar figure represents the actual worth of a share.

Mutual Fund Investors

The Investment Company Institute, a mutual fund industry trade group, released the first comprehensive study of mutual fund investors. Although fund assets have doubled in the past four years, the growth in investors has slowed. Here's a look at the results:

Figure #27
Households Owning Mutual Funds

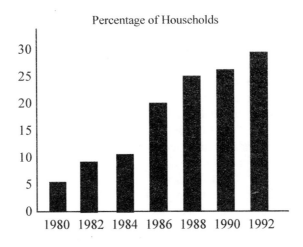

Percentage of Households

Figure #28
Number of Households Owning Mutual Funds

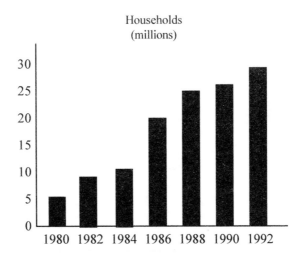

Households
(millions)

Figure #29
A Profile of Mutual Fund Investors

	Female	Male
Gender	44%	56%
Median Age	46	45
Median Household Income	$45,000	$53,000
Four-Year College Degree	45%	54%
Married	63%	79%
Widowed	12%	3%
Retired	24%	23%
Own an IRA	72%	74%
Financial Assets	$110,000	$116,000

Figure #30
New vs. Seasoned Mutual Fund Investors

One in ten fund shareholders bought fund shares for the first time after December 1990. How the newcomers compare with seasoned investors:

	New Investors	Seasoned Investors
Median Age	37	46
Median Household Income	$40,000	$50,000
Completed College	51%	50%
Retired	9%	25%
Own an IRA	55%	75%

Figure #31
Household Income of Mutual Fund Investors

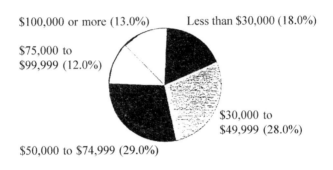

$100,000 or more (13.0%) Less than $30,000 (18.0%)

$75,000 to
$99,999 (12.0%)

$30,000 to
$49,999 (28.0%)

$50,000 to $74,999 (29.0%)

Why Invest In Mutual Funds?

A mutual fund is a practical and efficient way for people with similar goals to pool their money in an effort to achieve those goals. Whether the goals include funding education, beating inflation, preparing for retirement, or financing reachable dreams, the collective power of mutual fund dollars can open diverse investment opportunities that may be cost-prohibitive for many individual investors to do on their own.

The following is a discussion of the many advantages of fund participation.

A mutual fund is able to trade in tens of thousands of shares, while most of us — short of winning the lottery — will never personally possess the wealth required to play in such major leagues. Usually the fund can buy and sell large numbers of shares in a single transaction, as opposed to the generally limited purchasing power of the individual investor. This *economy of scale* can have the additional benefit of a reduced rate on brokerage commissions — as advantage that is passed on to the mutual fund shareholder.

A mutual fund is also able to trade in a wider variety of securities than most individuals. It is not uncommon for a fund to be invested in over 100 different securities, such as airlines, pharmaceuticals, electronics, utilities, chemicals, food, and steel. Such *diversification* reduces the risk inherent in having all of the eggs in one basket. Figures #32-#34 illustrate diversification of fund investment dollars, diversification by participation in more than one mutual fund, and diversification by participation in investments outside of mutual funds.

Figure #32
Fund Investors' Portfolio

Household financial assets of the average fund investor total $114,000, not counting real estate and employer-sponsored retirement plans. Of that, $43,500 is in funds. How fund assets break down:

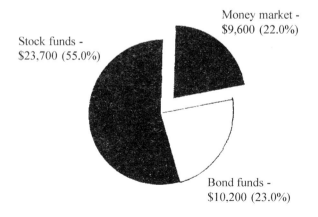

Money market -
$9,600 (22.0%)

Stock funds -
$23,700 (55.0%)

Bond funds -
$10,200 (23.0%)

Figure #33
Multiple Fund Participation Percentages

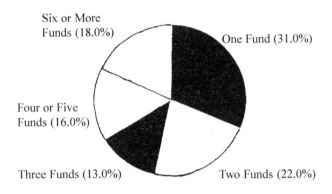

Six or More
Funds (18.0%)

One Fund (31.0%)

Four or Five
Funds (16.0%)

Three Funds (13.0%)

Two Funds (22.0%)

Figure #34
Percentage of Mutual Fund Investors in Other
Investments

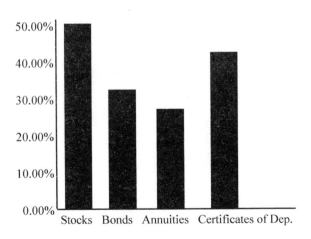

Although the investment should be considered long-term, mutual fund shares have very high liquidity. On any business day, the investor usually has the choice to redeem or cash in all or part of his fund shares. The amount he receives for his shares will represent a pro-rated share of the funds assets at that time. This could be more or less than the actual cost of the shares, depending on the investment performance of the fund.

By participating in a mutual fund, investors can take advantage of the very profitable practice of *dollar cost averaging*. This practice generally reduces the overall cost per share of an investment. Dollar cost averaging requires the individual to invest a fixed amount of money (of his own determination) on a regular basis. As a result of this systematic approach, investment dollars buy more shares when the price is down and less shares at a higher cost. Using a nice round figure of $100 invested on a quarterly basis, Figure #35 demonstrates the potential increase in account value when shares are purchased through dollar cost averaging. Notice how the average cost per share to the investor is significantly lower than the average price per share over the one-year period of the sample. In a manner of speaking, the dollar cost averager is able to do what smart shoppers do almost daily — to buy in quantity when items are "on sale."

While no particular mutual fund will guarantee specific returns, they generally outperform individual amateurs on a consistent basis. The specific advantages that make mutual fund investment an attractive alternative to personal portfolio management can be summarized as follows:

- *Economy of Scale*
- *Diversification*
- *Full-time, Professional Management*
- *Convenience*
- *Liquidity*
- *Dollar Cost Averaging*

146

Bradley Gummow

Figure #35
Dollar Cost Averaging

	Investment Amount	Share Price	Shares Purchased	Account Value
JAN	$100	$10.00	10	$100
APRIL	$100	$12.50	8	$225
JULY	$100	$ 5.00	20	$190
OCT	$100	$10.00	10	$480
TOTAL	$100	$37.50	48	$480

Average Price Per Share: $9.38
($37.50 divided by 4)
Your Average Cost Per Share: $8.33
($400 divided by 48)
Your Savings Per Share: $1.05

The example shows that by investing $100 every quarter we would have purchased a total of 48 shares at an average cost of $8.33. Note that when the share cost is lower we buy more, and vice versa. If, instead, we were to purchase 48 shares (12 per quarter) over the same period, our average cost would have been $9.38. Buying a set number of shares results in higher share cost because we buy just as many shares when the stock is expensive as when it is cheap.

**Investing is More Than Picking Stocks —
What to Consider in Making Mutual Fund Choices**

Ask six of your friends, and you may get six distinctly different pieces of advice on how to pick investment winners. When you consider a manner of selection or style of investment vehicles, chose experts with years of experience and solid track records that apply rules that have worked for them consistently over the long haul. One of these professionals with an excellent record is Julian Lerner. In 1968, Julian Lerner founded one of the most successful mutual funds in the United States. He put up $1,000 of his own money and convinced other investors to join him in the charter fund. Today, as senior vice president of Houston-based AIM Capital Management, Inc. (the company that bought out his fund), Lerner oversees a multi-billion dollar mutual fund portfolio.

A vice president of a brokerage firm was impressed with Lerner's exceptional success in guiding the fund to an average annual return of 17.3% over a fifteen-year period. He asked Lerner to speak at a conference about his methods for making his company one of the top performers in the country.

Here are Lerner's Rules — suggestions for successful investing.

When a stock's price drops below a certain price, get out. A rule of thumb is to get rid of it when it drops between 15-20% below its highest point (which is not necessarily the price at which you bought it). There are exceptions, of course, but the reasons must be pretty obvious and dramatic for keeping a stock that is so far below its highest point.

Maintain a sell discipline. Don't lose your capital. Stocks are not sentimental or otherwise precious family heirlooms. They are marketable commodities, and are valuable to you only as they represent money. Remember; you are in it for the money.

Use a reasonable method of stock selection. Look for companies where earnings are improving, revenues are increasing and they have a backlog of business. If you must follow fads, choose a relatively harmless area of your life. By bending to fashion fads, for instance, you run the risk of appearing foolish for a short period of time. If you follow fads in investing, however, you run

148

the risk of losing your money.

*Consistently apply the method of stock selection you have chosen, whether it be mathematical or astrological. Although it may hurt you in the short run, over the long-term it will work to your benefit. Lerner pointed out that in 1988 he picked Kroger and R.J. Reynolds and those two were taken over. However, his rules got him out of them before the takeover. Even so, while 1988 was not a great year, 1989 was a superior one. Modern Portfolio Theory reinforces the concept that is appropriate diversification of assets over time — not individual selections — that it yields the most dependable returns over time.

*Diversify your portfolio. Lerner suggests that you should never put more than 5% of your assets in one company.

*Get professional management. "Don't fall in love with your stocks," advises Lerner. You are in it for the exchange of money, not the exchange of affection. It is stressful enough to manage a romantic entanglement; who needs to get misty over stocks?

*Know the portfolio manager and his record. A good broker will offer you a wide range of investments and will not pressure you to buy every time you talk.

*Be patient. Investing is not a "get-rich-quick" scheme. How does this company perform in the context of the overall market? Remember that daily and short-term activities look more volatile than in the longer duration and broader view.

*Use common sense. Be at least as deliberate in your selection of an investment company as you are in other major purchases. Spend at least as much time and care as you would in buying a car.

*Remember; it's your money. Don't do anything you don't want to do with it.

With such a wide variety of available funds, I caution investors to avoid hybrid, specialty funds. In 1982, I learned a valuable lesson about fund selection. "Communication" and "information" were the buzzwords and the market in that area was sizzling. I put a lot of people's money in to that segment of the market, and — low and behold — guess what part of the stock market cooled? (It is my personal opinion that stock market forecasters were created to make fortunetellers look good.) So don't hogtie yourself to any one area; remember the lessons of diversification and a common-sense approach. While that particular fund eventually warmed up again and performed well, such things are exceptions, rather than the rule.

Available choices of mutual funds include the following:

1. Stock Funds
    a. Maximum Growth
    b. Income
    c. Income and Growth
    d. Long-term
    e. Global
    f. Foreign
    g. Single Country
    h. Small Capitalization
    i. Large Capitalization
2. Income Funds
    a. U.S. Government Securities
    b. Corporate Bonds
    c. Tax-free Municipal Bonds
    d. Global Bonds
3. Option Funds
4. Technology Funds
5. Communication Funds
6. Utility Stocks
7. Service Industries, etc.

Common stock funds, for example, offer a wide diversification of stocks, and this reduces the inherent risk of stock ownership. Stock market mutual funds should be considered long-term investments. They are only to be considered as a 4-5 year minimum investment in my opinion. Don't try to be a market timer with Mutual Funds. Stock market timers may disagree; however, performance over time backs up the diversification view. (In the overall hierarchy, market timers were created to make the forecasters look good — who, you will remember, were created to make fortunetellers look good.) Figure #36 illustrates that is on our side in returns on common stock mutual funds over a period of time.

Figure #36

Common Stock Performance -- 1941-1991
Ten Year Periods

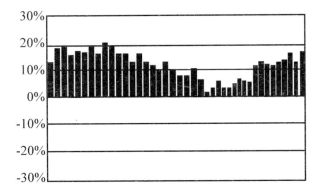

Income funds also offer a wide diversification of debt instruments, but beware of interest rates. If you believe that they will rise dramatically, you may want to avoid buying into a long-term bond fund.

Again, there are no guarantees that all mutual funds will be successful. But a diversified portfolio that is carefully selected by a systematic and rational approach will perform well over the long term to fund your obligations and desires.

I have been using an idea that I believe is better than mutual funds. Read on, to **Beat the Market**...

What You'll Learn

Do you feel you should earn more in the market? That your investments, funds, or stocks never seem to do quite as well as the market does?

The truth is that most investors do poorly and even 70% of the mutual funds fail to match the market.

In this brief report, you'll learn why most investors do not do very well with their investments. You will learn a system, which we now use for our clients, which has beaten the market for the last 25 years.

Most Investors Fail

Most investors have terrible performance in their portfolios. In fact, if you ask the average investor how much they earned last year, they have no idea. Yet, they will spend hours reading magazines with the cover story "Get the Best Funds for 1997". Or they will buy stocks they read about in a newsletter or heard about on the radio show or heard about from their brother-in-law.

It is no wonder that the average investor underperforms the market by so much.

152

A study by Dalbar, a leading mutual fund industry research firm, uncovered the following data. Their study measured investor performance in mutual funds for the 12 years ending December 31, 1997.

Investment Mechanism	Annual Return Achieved
Investors on their own	5.85%
Investors who used brokers	6.54%
Gain in the S & P 500	15.43%

For those twelve years, investors who invested on their own, did not even double their money, they earned a 97.9% return. Those investors who used brokers, did slightly better and a little more than doubled their money. But during these twelve years, the S & P increased by 460%! Investors in equity funds did not even come close!

Why is this?

The Two Problems:
Emotions and Opinions

Human beings are not cut out to be good investors. They make decisions emotionally, pulling money out of the market when they are afraid, putting money in when they feel comfortable. They hold investments that should be sold, not wanting to take a loss. They sell investments that should be held, afraid that the profit in their hands will disappear. In other words, investors violate a basic investing principal, "Cut your losses short, let your profits run."

I know this well from personal experience. During the last 15 years, I have worked with individual investors and have observed their investment "problems". Weekly, I have received calls from investors asking me about some article they read in the newspaper or something they heard on the news or some discussion in Congress that they felt could affect their investments. Invariably, these news items were bits of opinion, gossip, or some occurrence that would have no lasting affect on market direction. Even presidential elections have no effect on the stock market! (However, most investors who have not looked at the facts continue to think that the president does affect the market.)

The average investor is so influenced by their emotions and listening to other's opinions, that they are unable to make a plan and stick to it.

The second problem concerns limitations of the human mind. We can only pay attention to a few issues at the same time. Yet, there are hundreds of issues that affect the market. Just watch one edition of *Wall Street Week* and you will see "experts" spouting their opinions. "I think rates will rise…the market looks toppy…GNP growth is slowing down…employment growth is accelerating…" These are limited observations that are part of a very large picture that our human minds are unable to process. So we latch on to a few items that we can understand and these become our opinions, right or wrong.

There is a Solution

If the investor wants success, he must remove emotions and opinion from his investing. He must understand that two tools are needed to make money in the market:

1) **One must understand that the market requires patience.** An impatient or nervous person will get abused in the stock market.

Just look at what patience does for an investor:

	Chance of Making Money in the Stock Market*
In any One year	71%
In any Five years	84%
In any Ten years	97%
In any Fifteen years	100%

(*Based on actual results in the S & P 500 from 1926 through 1996.)

The patient investor who looks 10 to 15 years ahead can do very well. The nervous investor keeps asking, "Is the market too high? Do you think the Democrats will push the market down? What do you think Greenspan will do?"

The nervous investor is always focused on the latest news story and does not have a long-term view. Such an investor will be in and out of the market and lack the patience that the stock market demands to be a winner.

2) **You must have a system.** You will never make money without a preplanned system of investing. Without a system, you will be whipped around by your emotions when the market is moving. You will always be asking questions such as, "Should I buy now? Should I sell now? What should I buy now? What's a good investment now? Should I pull out of the market because it's too high?"

These are the questions of someone who has no plan and will never make a significant return in the market. Such a person is a gambler (and maybe doesn't even know it) and might be best off betting on the outcome of next weekend's football game.

The serious investor has a plan to follow.

A Plan to Follow

The Dow Dividend Strategy is such a plan. It has outperformed 75 % of the mutual funds tracked by Morningstar for the past 15 years. It has beaten the S & P 500 by 34% since 1972, turning $10,000 into $363,900. And it has done so with low risk. We have used this system for many delighted clients and continue to use it.

An investor who wants growth of principal with low risk and a plan for success must consider the Dow Dividend Strategy.

The Dow Dividend Strategy

The Dow Dividend Strategy calls for selecting the ten highest yielding stocks in the Dow Jones Industrial Average. An equal dollar amount is invested in each stock. These are held for one year.

At the end of the year, the portfolio is re-balanced so that the investor is again holding the 10 highest yielding stocks in the Dow Jones Industrial Average (in as close to equal amounts as is practical).

This procedure is repeated annually.

ALL NEWS, DIVIDEND CUTS OR INCREASES, ANNOUNCEMENTS, AND SPIN-OFFS ARE IGNORED. The portfolio is re-balanced only once per year.

The investor must ignore all sentiment, news, personal, likes and dislikes, and opinions about stocks.

For example, one of the best performers in the last few years has been Philip Morris. At the same time, the

156

average investor was convinced that holding tobacco stocks was the worst possible investment. This is a perfect example of bias leading the investor to an incorrect conclusion.

The following page shows results of the strategy compared to the entire Dow Jones Industrial Average and the S & P 500.

Most importantly, look at years when the market did really poorly such as 1973 and 1974. The Dow Dividend Strategy protected the investor's principal much better than the market. This system has given the investor a portfolio that has held its value better in down years, yet has outperformed the market and almost every mutual fund.

(Note: there is a version of this system using only 5 stocks which is not discussed in this report.)

Performance Dow Dividend Strategy
Annual Percentage Returns

Year	S & P 500	Dow Jones Industrial Average	Dow Dividend Strategy Ten	Dow Dividend Strategy Five
1973	-15	-13	-6	2
1974	-26	-24	-3	-6
1975	37	45	58	68
1976	24	23	36	41
1977	-7	-13	-4	6
1978	7	3	-3	1
1979	18	11	14	10
1980	32	22	25	41
1981	-5	-4	-5	4
1982	21	27	25	42
1983	23	26	31	36
1984	6	1	6	11
1985	32	34	32	30
1986	18	27	28	30
1987	5	6	6	11
1988	17	16	24	22
1989	31	33	27	10
1990	-3	-1	-8	-15
1991	30	24	36	62
1992	7	7	27	34
1993	10	17	27	34
1994	1	5	4	9
1995	37	36	36	30
1996	25	29	28	26
1997	33	25	22	20

158

Average Annual Return 1973-1997	13.00%	13.10%	18.20%	21.40%

Performance of Dow Dividend Strategy

SUMMARY

	S & P 500	Dow Jones Industrial Average	Dow Dividend Strategy Ten	Dow Dividend Strategy Five
Year				
Value Today of $10,000 invested January 1, 1973	$213,013	$216,811	$658,078	$1,269,396
Average Annual Return 1973-1996	13.00%	13.00%	18.30%	21.50%
Standard Deviation (Risk)	16.7	16.7	15.8	19.1
Risk Adjusted Return	0.78	0.78	1.16	1.12

I have never met one investor that was able to stick to this simple system. That is why we inexpensively manage portfolios for our investors using this strategy. Our fee is 1% to 2%.

It takes discipline to follow a plan and most people do not have that discipline. They need a professional to keep them on course. Some people are penny-wise and pound-foolish. They try and save the 1% to pay a professional and then they fail to use the system correctly and lose 3%, 5% or more each year in profits.

Chapter 6

Tax-Deferred Annuities

"Always try to rub up against money, for if you rub up against money long enough, some of it may rub off on you."

Damon Runyon

Annuities: What and Why?

Suppose that in 1968, you gazed into the crystal ball of American events. You saw the longest war in our history. You witnessed Watergate and watched a president resign in disgrace. Interest rates scaled record heights; bankruptcies followed suit. In the course of the longest bout of inflation ever, the view of Wall Street revealed the longest bear market ever, adjusted for inflation. Stock prices took the plunge. The convictions of Ivan Boesky, et al, cast another shadow on Wall Street. AIDS emerged as modern history's baffling plague. Even the weather refused to cooperate — leaving droughts to wreak their own brand of havoc. And then El Nino.

If you could possibly have seen this coming over the next three decades, where would you have put your money in 1968? You would have buried it in the backyard, right? Seriously, though, in spite of the combined assault of political, financial, and natural disasters, the best place to have invested your long-term money over the past two decades has been equities. Stocks are no place for short-term money, but if you want to eke out an extra two to three percentage points in your rates of return over the long haul, equities should definitely be a part of your diversified investment portfolio.

How do annuities fit into this picture? Annuities are probably one of the best long-term investments you can make in this tax environment. Although we don't have access to a crystal ball for a glimpse of the future economic panorama, we can readily see how annuities can provide significant funding for some of our long-range goals. The characteristics that make annuities attractive investments are their tax-deferred nature, the choice of fixed or variable types, the effects of compounding, extremely low risk, and relative safety of capital.

Tax acts in the 1980's and 90's removed many investments from tax-sheltered status. The annuity is one of few remaining under this protection. Current indications suggest that annuities will continue their sheltered status for the foreseeable future.

An annuity is a contract with an insurance company based on an investment that is made in a lump sum or in installments. There are three components to each annuity.

Annuitant. The person upon whose life the annuity is measured.

Owner. The person who owns the annuity, usually the annuitant.

Beneficiary. The person who receives the proceeds upon the death of the annuitant. Proceeds being defined as the account value.

The owner may begin to receive earnings from the annuity at the age of fifty-nine and a half. If he receives earnings prior to this, a 10% penalty on the growth will apply, in most cases. He may choose to annuitize — to immediately begin receiving regular monthly checks, in which case he will have to pay income taxes on the earnings immediately. The last in, first out accounting method is used.

Brokerage firms, investment houses, insurance companies, and some banks can provide you with annuities and can help you move them around. I also strongly suggest that you purchase annuities only from legal reserve insurance companies (those that have one dollar of current assets on hand for every dollar invested). This matching of asset and investment dollars is what helps to keep your money safe. To date, nobody has ever lost a dollar in a legal reserve insurance company fixed annuity that I know of. That doesn't mean it will never happen, but the risk is extremely small.

Figure #37 provides a graphic illustration of the benefits of tax deferment over both ten- and twenty-year periods. At the end of the twenty-year period, the taxable $100,000 investment has just about tripled. The tax-deferred investment is over four and a half times the original. In the latter case, not only is the initial investment earning interest, but the interest earned joins the principal in earning interest — without being diminished by immediate taxation.

Figure #37

Taxable vs. Tax-Deferred Investing

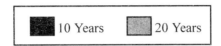

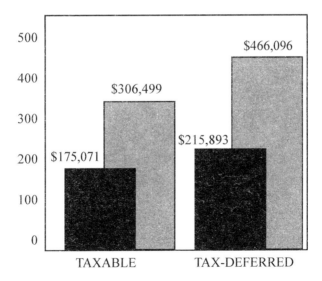

$100,000 initial investment, 8% pre-tax return, 28% tax bracket.

Types of Annuities

The fixed rate annuity provides a guarantee of principal and interest over a defined period of time. The investor may purchase an annuity through a single premium. He may, on the other hand, choose the flexible premium method, whereby the payment may be ongoing and additional premium payments are allowed at the owner's discretion.

When you hear the word premium, you may be thinking, "Oh, no! Insurance by any other name!" Don't panic. An annuity is sold by the insurance company, but it is not designed as a hedge against a variety or disasters. Unlike life insurance, it is designed to fund your long-term goals — not your funeral or the expenses of your heirs. Think of it as a certificate of deposit sold by an insurance company, with tax advantages. (One should note that certificates of deposit are FDIC insured up to $100,000 per account.

The fixed rate annuity does, in fact, act much like a certificate of deposit. Both have a predetermined duration, with a uniform interest rate throughout. One important difference is this: while the earnings from your annuity are remaining in your account and compounding for your benefit, the earnings on your certificate of deposit are immediately eligible for "Uncle Sam's profit sharing plan" at the highest marginal tax rate. This is especially significant when interest rates are low, as they are now.

When you reap the benefits of your annuity, you will probably be retired and, therefore, most likely be in a lower tax bracket. (If you are going to remain in the same bracket in retirement, you are doing better than most of us, so why on earth are you still working?)

The variable annuity offers all the benefits of mutual fund investing with all the tax advantages of a fixed rate annuity. Through the variable rate annuity, you can enjoy the gains of the stock, bond, or money market investments with a great big tax-deferred wrapper around them. While a portion of the gains from your stocks, bonds, and money market investments travel the federal river-of-no-return on April 15, your variable annuity blossoms in its shelter. It can even be transferred to another annuity as often as you like (called a 1035 exchange) without incurring any taxable consequences until you take the money out.

Figures #38 illustrates the tax-deferred advantages of the variable annuity. It compares the performance of the annuity to the independent mutual fund investment over a twenty-year period. The results are dramatic.

Figure #39 illustrates the tax-exempt transfer of annuities in contrast to the tax-liable movement of investments without the shelter. If you have old annuities, (over 5-7 years), consider a 1035 (tax-free), exchange to a newer one.

Figure #38

Annuities vs. Mutual Funds

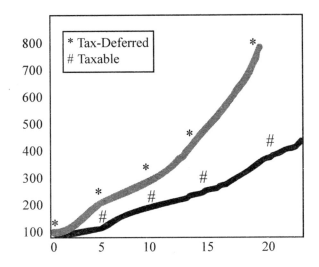

$100,000 initial investment, 12% pre-tax return, 3.5% mutual fund front load, 1.25% variable annuity mortality expense charge, 28% tax bracket.

Figure #39

Transferring Money

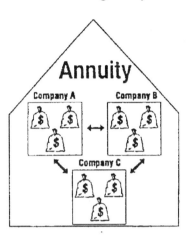

1035 Exchange: Money may be transferred between annuities without incurring current taxation.

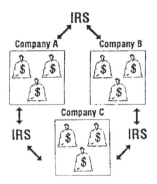

When money is transferred between investments, capital gains will be taxed along with current income.

Other Considerations in Annuity Investing

One of the ways to be involved in a variable annuity is buying into an asset manager portfolio. In this situation, a professional money manager will regularly adjust the distribution of assets to take maximum advantage of economic cycles. In other words, he may have money in stocks when the climate dictates, then move it to bonds when he feels the advantages are there. Within the bond area, he may choose U.S. Government issues one day and international another.

I don't mean to give the impression that shifts are made on a daily basis in an asset manager portfolio; however, adjustments in the matrix will be made with whatever frequency is necessary to ride the most profitable waves in the economic cycle. It is also important to note that while you as the investor are not initiating the decision-making process to switch from one particular investment to another, you do retain veto or override power. For example, you have the option of saying, "I don't want my money in stocks; stay on the bond side."

If you are going to invest in an asset manager portfolio, you would be wise to research who the money manager is. Since you will not be making the day-to-day decisions, you should feel confident in the one who is. In the final chapter, I will discuss selection of a professional money manager in more detail.

Along the lines of confidence in financial acumen, a friend of mine who is with the Fidelity Group — one of my favorite firms for variable annuity money management — shared with me this story from one of Peter Lynch's books. Lynch spoke to a group of seventh-graders from St. Agnes School near Boston about stock selection. Over a two-year period, this group of kids outperformed ninety-eight percent of Wall Street's money managers.

What was their secret? They used an intricate system that often escapes the adult mind. They all wanted to go to Disneyland, so they bought Disney. They all like eating at McDonald's, so they bought McDonald's. This was the kid's version of open-air analysis, which says that if it appears to be busy and working, it's probably profitable. Since this particular class had to go on to high school and eventually on with their lives, they are not available to manage your investments. So you will have to make your choice from among the Wall Street MBA gurus who, in most cases, finished behind them in the stock selection process. But you can learn a lesson from them: Keep it simple.

Now that I have bolstered your confidence in the ability of professionals to manage your annuity investments, I'll mention several other important considerations of the annuity field.

As I mentioned earlier, earnings received before the age of fifty-nine and a half are generally subject to a 10% tax penalty. If you die, you escape the penalty, but that's a rather extreme evasion technique. Should you exercise this option, however, it may be a comfort to know that your beneficiary will avoid probate costs and receive the total account value or the sum of all deposits, less any prior distribution, whichever is greater.

In the more popular option of surviving to receive the return on your annuity investment, distribution at any time will be considered earnings first. Accountants call this the LIFO method, which stands for last in, first out. For annuities prior to 1982, the principal is withdrawn first. Pay close attention to how the taxman fits into this scenario to help it work to your benefit.

If an annuity is placed in a qualified plan, you can use it for an IRA. In this case, all distributions are taxable.

Corporations may own annuities but are not eligible

Bradley Gummow

for the tax deferral available to individuals.

Summary of Advantages

Tax Deferral: No taxes are due on annuity earnings until they are withdrawn. While you will eventually have to pay taxes, the longer you wait to share with Uncle Sam, the more money you will have at the end of the annuity's duration. Remember tax-deferred compounding. In addition, you will likely be in a lower tax bracket when you have to part with a portion of the earnings.

1035 Exchange: Proceeds from one annuity may be transferred to another annuity and still retain tax-deferred status when the transaction is done through a 1035 exchange. There is no tax on the capital gains that result from the transfer. Appropriate paperwork must be submitted with the new application.

Death Benefit: Since you put the money in the annuity, it is certainly not to your benefit to die before you collect. Should this be the case, however, there are advantages for your beneficiary. He will be able to take the money out without any fee or discount to the price, generally. He will receive the current value of the investment. The annuity bypasses the probate process as well, resulting in savings of 2% to 8% of the assets and expedient distribution.

Extremely Low Risk: In a fixed rate annuity, your principal is absolutely secure. How it will weather inflation is of some concern, but the income from it will be regular and uniform, much like a CD. The variable annuity acts like a mutual fund investment, but without the immediate tax returns. Over the long term, the investment performs well.

Remember to have your broker review all annuities 5 years and older.

171

Chapter 7

Direct Investments & Real Estate

"Buy on the cannons; sell on the trumpets."

Baron Guv Rothschild

Bradley Gummow

Direct Investments and Limited Partnerships

Direct investments provide a way for individuals to invest in specific assets or operating businesses. They offer an innovative and tax-efficient way for individuals to participate in what everyone hopes will be the appreciation of the assets and businesses. As in the case of the mutual fund, investors with modest funds are able to participate in larger projects traditionally available only to institutions and the wealthiest investors. Among the most common direct investment avenues are real estate, equipment leasing, and oil and gas. Others available include cable television, research and development, and movies.

Most direct investments are structured as limited partnerships to avoid double taxation. Gains, losses, and all tax benefits are passed on directly to the limited partners.

Each limited partnership will have its own objective or reason of being. Before becoming involved with one, an investor must decide whether or not his objectives are compatible with those of the partnership.

In all fairness, I must point out here that the information that follows is a very brief review of limited partnerships. The cursory treatment given here will not provide enough background for you to determine the merits of one specific investment over another. I would not feel comfortable considering a limited partner investment — on either a personal or professional level — until I had examined a complete prospectus of a proposed partnership. Furthermore, if you sense that the limited treatment here reflects a value judgement on the merits of limited partnership as an investment vehicle, you are correct. I do feel you ought to be aware of them; however, I caution you to also beware of them.

In the same spirit of fairness I mentioned above, I feel obligated to share my feelings about the general concept of limited partnership, developed over a number of years of experience in the investment field. For the record, I have yet to be involved in a limited partnership that has worked as well as it was conceived and intended to work.

I have heard every story imaginable on how great oil and gas limited partnerships are. In my experience, however, the wealth of stories is far greater than any wealth earned from such an investment. Research and development limited partnerships are, in my opinion, designed to part people with their money. If it is in your heart to act as a patron, you might consider one. If financial gain is your motive, you'd be well advised to look elsewhere. Of course, if you were in the partnership that came up with Ibuprofen, you would have been a delighted exception to the rule — just like the stock picker who stumbled on Apple Computer or Walmart in their infancy.

A few cable television ventures have worked out rather well, but that has been the exception to the rule in the area of limited partnerships. Movie limited partnerships might have some potential if you have, for example, Clint Eastwood on board, and the box office is all but guaranteed. However, those in Mr. Eastwood's league are seldom lacking in backers. Your film, on the other hand, will most likely feature a less stellar cast and a more glaring risk. As in the case of research and development, you may end up extending charity; then again, it may work out. Can you afford to take that risk with your money?

Limited Partnership
Achieving Together What You Couldn't Achieve Alone

Individual ownership of real estate investment property is beyond the means of many Americans. It brings with it many operating and management responsibilities, as well as a need for regular attention, for which few people have the knowledge or time to deal with properly.

Accordingly, real estate limited partnerships are increasingly becoming part of the investor's financial portfolio.

In 1977, limited partnership offerings submitted to the National Association of Securities Dealers for review amounted to an aggregate $293 million. In 1983, that dollar amount had increased by 1,504% to $4.7 billion. Clearly, affordability, diversification, lack of management responsibility, and limited liability inherent in the limited partnership form of investment have created an increasing public demand for this product.

A real estate limited partnership can offer an excellent vehicle for participation in investment opportunities in real estate today. A limited partnership, consisting of at least one general partner (investors), is a legal entity formed for business or investment purposes. The general partner is the active partner responsible for administering the partnership.

The limited partner is a passive investor who participates in real estate ownership without the responsibility for management, the obligation for additional investment into the partnership, or incurring any partnership debts beyond the amount of the limited partner's original investment.

The advantages of investing through a limited partnership include:

1. *Increased purchasing power.* By pooling the funds of many investors, the partnership is able to purchase more and/or larger properties, often on more attractive terms than might otherwise be available to the individual investor.
2. *Diversification of investment.* The success of the

investment is not dependent upon the performance of any one property. A given partnership seeks to acquire a portfolio of properties in geographically diversified locations, thus spreading an investor's capital among all of the properties.

3. *Economies of scale.* The partnership is able to significantly reduce ongoing operating expenses by spreading the cost among many properties.

4. *Professional management.* The general partner frees the investor from the task of acquisition, day-to-day management, bookkeeping, and sales, and places these responsibilities in the hands of skilled professionals. Value is directly related to the partnership's ability to generate net operating income during the holding period.

5. *Administration.* The general partner is responsible for the preparation of partnership tax returns and record keeping.

6. *Limited liability.* The limited partners generally are not liable for partnership debts and obligations beyond the amount of their original capital contribution. Check the prospectus for future potential assessments.

7. *Tax deductions.* A limited partnership does not pay taxes on its earnings. Therefore, all of the tax benefits of ownership of real estate flow through to the partners. This benefits the investor by generally creating sufficient deductions to defer tax liability on cash distributions until the sale. At that time the gain is generally taxed at the more favorable capital gains tax rate. Excess deductions may be used to reduce the tax burden of income from other sources.

Common Types of Limited Partnerships

1) Real Estate - Public Limited Partnerships
Objective 1: Capital Appreciation
Objective 2: Tax Write-Offs. Depreciation creating tax loss to offset other capital growth.
Objective 3: If program is leveraged, your appreciation is based on both your initial investment and proportionate shares of funds borrowed.

Popular real estate investments include luxury garden-style apartment complexes and mini-warehouses. These are income oriented.

2) Oil and Gas Limited Partnerships
Objectives vary depending on whether the partnership is an income fund, drilling, exploratory, or combination of all three.

Tax advantages come from depletion allowances, depreciation, and drilling expenses. Exploratory and especially Wild Cat Exploration Funds usually involve the highest risk, highest write-offs, and highest reward potentials. Their motto: You can't steal second base by keeping your foot on first.

3) Cable T.V. Limited Partnerships

Partnerships acquire existing systems or build new ones with the principle objective of selling the system at a gain in the future. Partnerships can be leveraged. Systems will usually add new services, i.e. burglar alarm systems, fire and smoke detection, shop-at-home services, games, and additional features.

4) Research and Development Limited Partnerships

A method of raising capital for proposed inventions or new product development.

5) Movie Limited Partnerships

Raising capital for the production and distribution of motion pictures.

Finally, ask yourself these questions before committing to a limited partnership course:

1) Does it meet my objectives? Most likely, at least one of your objectives is financial gain, either through earnings or growth. Will the projected partnership result in the returns you need? Are you comfortable with an investment in which you have little or no control?

2) Do the tax advantages fit my particular tax profile? The Tax Reform Act of 1986 had a profound effect on the ability of limited partnerships to meet some of their intended tax advantages. Like any other investment, the limited partnership must be viewed in the context of a "partner" in the diversified portfolio. Make sure you understand the tax impact in conjunction with your other investments

3) How liquid is the limited partnership investment? Chances are, the answer is not very, or not at all. These are typically long-term, and most often you will not find anyone waiting in line to buy your share at a fair value.

**4) Does the risk/reward profile fit my investment

style? Compare it to the other types in your portfolio to see if it has a place.

Real Estate

Since the early days of our nation's history, real estate has been one of America's most popular and profitable investments. In one of our most beloved stories, an earnest father tells his willful daughter, "Land's the only thing that matters, Katie Scarlett." And from the first homesteaders to the first-time homebuyers of today, land acquisition has been both a necessity and a passion.

When we look at real estate as an investment category, we need to look beyond the structure and piece of earth we call home. We will always need a place to live, so I do not recommend considering your home an investment vehicle. We also need to consider real estate as a long-term investment, so we should not be putting any money into it that we may need in a hurry or for an emergency.

Why buy real estate? Will Rogers' reply was simple and sensible: "They ain't making any more of it."

Franklin Roosevelt maintained, "Managed with some reasonable care, it is one of the safest investments in the world."

According to the October 1982 issue of *Commercial Investment Council*, "Apartment buildings are the best real estate investment for investors looking for stable growth in the future."

Periods of moderate inflation and moderate economic growth generally affect real estate and other direct investments in a positive manner. For the most part, real estate does not like rampant inflation. During the mid to late 1970's and early 1980's, farmland prices were rising with inflation. What happened suddenly? Boom! Property values took the plunge. Don't forget to watch for the

179

grim reaper of inflation as you time your real estate transactions. Keep in mind that what goes up must also go down, and vice versa.

Let's look at how to structure a real estate purchase so that it can achieve our goals. Assume, for example, we are going to buy a $100,000 piece of property. If we are cash rich at the time of the purchase, and we pay for it outright, what does that do to the income from the property? It increases it, of course, because we don't have a mortgage payment. If our goal is income oriented, then, we are going to go into a property that is leveraged either very lightly or not at all.

How should we structure a real estate purchase if we are tax oriented? This time, mortgage payments work in our favor, so we will initially put down as little as possible to be tax advantaged.

Another factor that makes real estate an attractive investment is the concept of depreciation in the value of rental properties. While the 1986 tax reforms extended the period of depreciation from nineteen to a much longer period, there is still some tax advantage. Depreciation is, after all, a non-cash expense.

The stories about the plight of farmers notwithstanding, real estate continues to be the good investment it has been historically. Ask a successful farmer how he did last year, and you may get that wistful look — even as he stares you down from the window of his new $40,000 pickup truck. While he maintains he has never had a good year, his new Cadillac sits in the garage behind him.

In our current economic climate, real estate continues its traditional popularity as an investment vehicle when property is well selected and managed. From all indications, it is a trend that will continue into the next century. According to recent figures published by the IRS, the wealthiest Americans — based on estates valued over $350,000 in 1996 — invest in real estate.

Figure #40

How the USA's Wealthy Invest

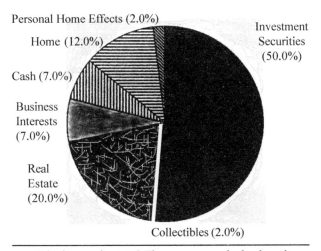

Personal Home Effects (2.0%)

Home (12.0%)

Cash (7.0%)

Business Interests (7.0%)

Real Estate (20.0%)

Investment Securities (50.0%)

Collectibles (2.0%)

Why buy real estate? The answer can be broken down into ten key reasons.

1) *Track record of success vs. traditional investments.*
2) *Basic fundamental need.*
3) *Supply/demand relationship is favorable.*
4) *"Affordability Crisis" (high cost of home ownership).*
5) *Changing lifestyles/smaller household formations.*
6) *Shortfall of new housing starts.*
7) *Expensive replacement costs.*
8) *Favorable tax treatment.*
9) *Inflation hedge.*
10) *Historically, not as volatile as other more traditional investments.*

The four primary benefits of ownership in real estate are:

1) *Appreciation (increase net worth).*
2) *Tax benefits.*
3) *Cash flow.*
4) *Equity build up (mortgage reduction).*

Property Management

If you decide to become involved in a real estate limited partnership, you must realize that it is a more complicated issue than mere acquisition of property. Active, astute, and regular management will determine whether or not you will realize a return on your investment. Although, as I mentioned previously, you give up control to a general partner in this type of investment, you obviously have control over two overriding principles: the decision of whether or not to invest, and the choice of the particular limited partnership. To protect your investment dollars, open your eyes before you open your wallet, and make a fully informed choice.

Involvement... The Difference Between Words and Action

Talking about profitability doesn't make it happen. Most real estate syndicators believe management of a partnership's properties is every bit as important as the acquisition of the properties themselves.

Property management is entrusted with the responsibility of implementing the strategy of the partnership. Management is perhaps the most vital single factor in determining whether or not an investment will be profitable and to what degree.

Bradley Gummow

By definition, *managing real estate is the business of preserving and enhancing the value of the partnership's properties while expanding its capacity to generate income.*

Revenue Enhancement

Revenue enhancements are a continuous goal for the property management staff. It begins with actively seeking residents for the properties and retaining them so that occupancy levels remain high. Comparable properties are monitored on a regular basis, and rental prices are constantly evaluated. Revenue enhancement also includes establishing rental policies and ensuring that rents are paid on time. As rental income is received, it is placed in a high-yielding, short-term investment account.

REIT's, Real Estate Investment Trusts

Many individuals lack the resources to adequately diversify in real estate investing. Property management can be very demanding and the purchase can require a substantial commitment to make it easier, consider REIT's, Real Estate Investment Trusts. In essence, a REIT is a corporation, many of which trade on the NYSE, that act similar to a mutual fund. That is, they "pool" the monies of many investors to acquire real estate for investment purposes. These real estate "professionals" then manage the properties for shareholders, like you and me. Because they trade like a regular stock, you have <u>instant</u> liquidity. I believe REIT's offer lots of advantages:
1) Professional management
2) Instant liquidity
3) Current income in the form of dividends — stable income
4) Appreciation potential

183

5) Instant Diversification

Most REIT's specialize, either geographically or by type of property. Types of property could include:
1) Office buildings
2) Apartment complexes
3) Industrial Properties
4) Hotels
5) Health care
6) Shopping centers
7) Storage facilities
8) Prisons

Prisons are interesting, they rent the prisons to states (good customers) and prisons tend to be recession proof. Unfortunately, there is no shortage of bad people to occupy them.

REIT's are required by law to distribute 95% of earnings. If earnings increase you get a "raise" in income. Conversely, if there is an over-supply of your kind of properly, dividends could be lowered. Approximately, as of this writing, 25% of a dividend is tax-free, due to the depreciation laws. This, of course lowers your cost basis — meaning you will get taxed at a long-term capital gains when the REIT is sold.

REIT's happen to be my favorite way to participate in real estate, given past track records and instant liquidity coupled with good income.

Chapter 8

Tangible Investments

"Never invest in anything that eats or needs painting."

Billy Rose

Tangible investments are extremely speculative, and are generally more feasible for younger investors who will be exposed to many economic cycles. They can be excellent hedges against rampant inflation and severe economic downturn.

Tangible assets may include gold, silver, or other precious metals, gems, coins, art, stamps, or memorabilia from an infinite variety of areas of interest. With so many possibilities — each having its own intricate value system — this is one area where I recommend expert evaluation and advice.

We are going to take the Bill Sawyer approach to tangible investments in this chapter. I apprenticed under Bill when I got started in the investment business, and in all of my years of experience, I have yet to find a more direct, concise approach to investing.

According to Bill Sawyer, tangible assets — specifically precious metals such as gold, silver, and platinum — love random political events and rampant inflation. In other words, precious metals perform best during unpredictable politics and explosive inflation.

Some folks even use gold and silver prices as forecasters of inflation. When those prices start to rise, they believe inflation will follow suit. The statistical correlation between the two is, in fact, historical. Compare gold prices to the prime rate of interest for the years 1982 and 1998:

	1982	1998
Gold	$675 per ounce	$300 per ounce
Prime Rate	18%	8.5%

Some financial advisors will argue that you may want to have five percent of your investments in precious metals as a kind of inflation hedge. You might think of it as an insurance policy that you hope you don't need.

186

When the rate of inflation rises, what happens to your bond value? The value of your CD's? Your purchasing power? All these areas decline dramatically; so do real estate values and stocks.

Unless, however, your crystal ball shows even more random political events than we have seen over the past five years, you might want to avoid gold and silver as investments.

For my own money, I do not care for the volatile nature of tangible investments, and I don't have the time or inclination to do the research necessary to make them profitable. An exception is "hedging" your portfolio with a good gold fund, during an inflationary economic cycle. They are long term, have a limited market and require a great deal of specialized understanding. I normally recommend 3%-5% of an investor's portfolio be placed in a good gold fund.

As in every area, there are exceptions to the general rule. I hear that tiny ceramics have outperformed stocks as an investment area over the last fifty years. Certain tangibles other than precious metals have also done well. But as a small percentage of your total portfolio, I question whether the time investment that must be made in dealing with this area yields adequate returns for the effort.

If you decide to become involved in this area, I feel qualified to make only these two suggestions: be cautious and seek credible guidance.

Chapter 9

Part 1 - Insurance: Life and Disability

Part 2 - Long-Term Care Insurance

"I've got all the money I'll ever need...if I die by four o'clock."

Henny Youngman

Bradley Gummow

Insurance: a Necessary Evil

None of us needs to compound personal tragedy with economic catastrophe. As a result, the insurance industry permeates almost every aspect of our modern lives. In America, we can be covered from the moment of our conception to our time of expiration. An infinite variety of policies offer to protect everything from our health, possessions, and potential to our liabilities and lives.

It would be impossible to cover all the insurance bases in a book of this nature; even a brief treatment of health insurance alone could fill a book. The industry has been under intense scrutiny in recent years. The need for a major overhaul of the health care industry was an issue that received plenty of attention in the recent round of national campaigns.

If you haven't been made painfully aware of the problem on a personal level, Figure #41 will give you some indication of why the cost of health care has captured so much attention. Over the ten-year period between 1980 and 1990, the Medical Care Price Index surpassed the Consumer Price Index early on, and by the end of the decade had doubled the increases of the CPI.

Since the topic of health insurance receives almost daily coverage on a national level and sweeping changes may be brewing, I won't treat it here — other than this brief reminder of the devastation that can result from lack of it. I have seen many fine estates ruined from lasting medical bills.

In this chapter, I will discuss in more detail, two types of insurance coverage that I believe have major impact on your ability to meet your financial future without fear: life and disability. You may find the rationale for having them to be, at best, unpleasant; nevertheless, the consequences for not having them can be, at worst, catastrophic.

189

Life insurance and disability insurance are designed to mitigate varying degrees of disaster by protecting your family's financial way of life in times of loss. Of these two, I will give more extensive attention to disability insurance. Not only is it less understood; people are more likely to be caught in a bind without adequate disability insurance than they are to be caught without enough life insurance.

Before I treat either type specifically, I would like to make a few general comments about purchasing insurance. First, if you are a careful consumer, you look for a good value on an item that suits your needs. Selecting appropriate insurance is no different. You must determine exactly what kind and how much you need before you begin to shop for insurance.

Don't let the salesperson tell you what you need; he works on commission. Many of us couldn't wait to buy microwave ovens when the technology was new. Did you buy the one that did everything but change the baby's diapers, only to discover that, eventually, all you used it for was reheating coffee and leftovers?

How can you decide just how much insurance you need? Worksheets 8 and 9 that follow will help you quantify your income and expenditures in the event of the loss of a wage earner. As you fill them out now, you will begin to have an idea of how your budget will be affected by a reduction in your work force. Figure #42 projects the percentage of your previous income you will need to maintain your standard of living after the loss of a wage earner.

Bradley Gummow

Figure #41
Escalating Medical Care Costs

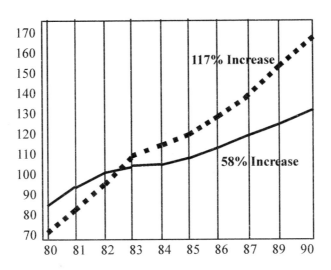

117% Increase

58% Increase

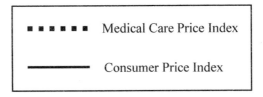

■ ■ ■ ■ ■ ■ Medical Care Price Index

————— Consumer Price Index

191

Worksheet #8
Income Needs

1. Income: Combined income of wage earners.   _____

2. Income Objectives: Annual income needed after death of wage earner (See figure #41).   _____

3. Survivor's Social Security Benefits: If no minor children, use zero.   _____

4. Income Shortage Subtotal: Subtract line 3 from line 2.   _____

5. Other Income: This includes income from the other spouse when both work, trust income, and income producing property not included in line 8 of cash needs worksheet.   _____

6. Total Anuual Income Shortages: This is the amount of annual income to be replaced. Subtract line 5 from line 4.   _____

7. Endowment Required: Amount of life insurance needed to provide this income; derived income shortage (line 6) by a projected interest rate. Use 7% rate as a conservative estimate, but raise the rate if you expect the survivors to use some principal.   _____

8. Cash Requirements: Amount from line 9, *Cash Needs Worksheet*. Note if negative amount.   _____

192

Bradley Gummow

Worksheet #9
Cash Needs

1. Immediate Money Funds: To pay bills presented after death, such as medical and hospital expenses, funeral expenses, attorney and executor fees, federal and estate taxes, and probate court costs. _____

2. Debt Liquidation: Amount needed to pay installment credit, unpaid notes, school and auto loans, and bills. _____

3. Emergency Funds: For unexpected bills not readily payable from current income; auto or home repairs, medical bills. _____

4. Mortgage/Rent Payment Fund (optional): Some families plan to pay off the mortgage if the insured person dies, so the survivors have a debt-free home. _____

5. Child/Home Care Fund (optional): To pay for new expenses created as a spouse formerly performing these duties without any cash outlay. _____

6. Educational Fund: The costs of a four-year undergraduate education vary, but $20,000 per child is usually the minimum that should be provided. _____

7. Subtotals: Add line 1 through 6. _____

8. Available Assets: Such as savings and existing life insurance, including amount provided by employer. _____

9. Cash Needs Requirements: Subtract line 8 from line 7. If line 8 exceeds line 7, note negative amount. _____

193

Figure #42

Income Objective Upon Loss of a Wage Earner

Based on a study by the Bureau of Labor Statistics, the following are typical income objectives in order to permit a family to maintain a standard of living after the death of the wage earner. Assumption is the mortgage of residence is paid, or rent fund has been established, and educational expenses are provided for separately.

Annual Gross Income	% of Gross Income Required
Up to $35,000	70%
$35,001 - $39,000	66%
$39,001 - $43,001	63%
$43,001 - $48,000	60%
Over $48,000	57%

Now that you have a better idea of how much insurance you'll need, where should you get it? Like any other business, the insurance business has its share of winners and losers. Fortunately, you won't have to rely on rumor or your intuition for evidence of an insurance company's dependability.

Insurance companies are rated by a number of independent agencies. These ratings reflect the companies' abilities to pay claims. Since the ability to pay claims is exactly what you need from an insurance company, its rating should be an overriding concern in making your choice. With the variety of insurance companies approaching the number of breakfast cereals on the market, you should have no problem finding one to meet your needs that has at least an "A+" rating.

The following companies are the three primary rating agencies for the insurance industry: A.M. Best Company, Standard & Poor's Corporation, and Moody's. Ratings are updated periodically.

In summary, determine your needs before you make your insurance purchase. Then make your choice from among the highly rated companies who offer plans to suit your personal profile.

Life Insurance

No matter which angle you approach it from, the subject of life insurance has rather gruesome overtones. In fact, if it is your policy, you might more appropriately think of it as death insurance because its purpose is to protect your survivors when you expire before your financial obligations do.

In the process of the sale of a life insurance policy, two parties approach the transaction from basically opposing philosophies. The buyer's view is, "Oh my God, I could die tomorrow, and my family will be forced to forage through dumpsters for their dinners."

The insurance company is thinking, "Nah, you'll live long enough to drive your kids crazy while we get rich investing your premiums." And, quite frankly, if the odds were not with them, they would not be around to capitalize on your fears of mortality.

Nevertheless, who would be the first to stand up and risk his family's future? So call it a necessary evil. Let's see how it fits in with our total investment picture.

First of all, it is an investment that will probably never

pan out for the insured personally. Your actuarial life expectancy is the basis of your policy. If you live a long, prosperous life, a third party (the insurance company) will derive more financial benefit from your invested dollars than you, and your beneficiary will collect the payout. If you die early on, you won't be taking it with you either. You will have paid less in premiums; so besides an earlier payout to your beneficiary, your estate may have a bit more cash on hand, as well.

Viewed in this context, then, what is the most prudent course to take in purchasing life insurance? My recommendation is two fold. Number one: buy the cheapest term life insurance you can find. (You don't need a chainsaw to cut a cheesecake.) We are getting a rude lesson about all the fancy universal life and other options, now that interest rates have dropped. You want to stay in control of your investment dollars and have the opportunity to reap the benefits of the economic cycles yourself.

Number two: keep your life insurance at the highest level when your children are young. That is when your financial responsibility for their present and potential needs looms largest. If your mortgage is new, and you have car payments and other installment debts, you need more insurance than when you are single, childless, or debt-free.

How much is enough? Review your completed Worksheets 8 and 9. Consider both immediate and long-term expenses that your family will face without you. Liquidating cumbersome installment debts, paying estate taxes, making the home debt-free, and funding children's care and education are among the more expensive obligations your family may have.

Review your life insurance every now and then and make adjustments when necessary. Once your children are gainfully employed, your mortgage is retired and you are relatively free of installment debt, the money you paid on larger premiums will work better for you elsewhere.

Several years ago, rates for life insurance were lowered — a pleasant departure from the general trend in insurance rates. Since there is plenty of competition in this climate, you will have plenty of choice if you are shopping. Comparison shop. Get what you need at the best price available.

I advise you to have a professional life insurance analysis done, which a broker should perform at no cost to you. This will reveal if you can do any of the following:

1) Build up cash values to a benefit faster.
2) Get more protection for the same cost.
3) Pay less for the same coverage.
4) Consolidate policies to save on premiums and/ or paperwork.

Disability Insurance

By the time we reach adulthood, most of us have admitted to ourselves that we are going to die sometime. Most of us have even taken some steps to provide for that eventuality by purchasing the life insurance we discussed in the previous section. In our most productive years, however, we are actually more likely to suffer some degree of disability than we are to drop dead. And if we are not prepared with financial backup to carry us through times of disability, we may have cause to wish for the latter.

Most of us have also taken steps to insure what we feel are our most valuable assets. We insure our homes and expensive possessions — anything that we have paid for with our hard-earned cash and would not want to lose. As we dish out more of our hard-earned cash to protect

197

our highly prized possessions, we often forget to protect the thing that enabled us to obtain them: our ability to work. It is this ability that enables us to earn money to provide for our wants and desires. The loss of this ability puts everything we have worked for at risk.

Anyone who has been out of work at any time has already learned an important lesson: in most cases, expenses continue even when the paychecks cease. So, what kind of disability coverage will you need to cover your expenses in the event you are unable to perform your job? If you have done your homework as you have read this book, you have determined already what those expenses are. You are ready, therefore, to evaluate what specific provisions a disability policy should include to protect your income in the manner you require.

The following article from *Dental Economics* gives as clear an explanation of disability insurance as any I've seen. While it focuses specifically on dentistry, it addresses universal issues that apply to any career.

---

* The following article was reprinted with permission from the February 1986 issue of *Dental Economics*. Permission not to be construed as an endorsement of any product or service.

Plan to protect your most valuable practice asset -- yourself

by Barry H. Josselson, Attorney

Dentists uniformly admit that disability insurance is an important form of protection. However, your finding the right disability policy requires your knowing what questions to ask and what features to look for.

Naturally, long-term disability is something you don't even like to think about, much less plan for. I'm not going to worry about it, you say. If it happens, it happens! But by challenging the probability that you'll be one of those dentists who suffers a serious illness or injury before reaching 65, you're fighting steep odds that put your whole way of life at risk.

Statistics tell a sobering story:

- A 35-year old dentist has a greater chance of becoming seriously disabled than he or she does of dying before reaching age 65.
- About one-third of all 35-year old dentists will be disabled for three months or longer before they reach 65.
- Long-term disabilities rank as leading factors in mortgage foreclosures as well as in personal bankruptcy filings.

"So what?" Well, if your income stops or drops drastically when you cannot work, and your personal and business expenses continue and perhaps even increase, a disability is calamitous. In that event, your life insurance will not be of any help — unless you decide to borrow cash from it; in which case, this will leave your family vulnerable. If your retirement plan becomes your means of support, you are using it for the wrong reason. Moreover, it had better be sufficiently funded to carry you for a long period of time.

As a dentist, you have much more to lose by a disability than most other professional or business people. An arm, back, or leg injury that would merely inconvenience an attorney, a CPA, or a small business owner can put you completely out of service; and most importantly, unlike the business owner, your income terminates abruptly and completely unless you individually, can unlock the door to your office and apply your professional skills to your patients. That is why a quality, individual disability income policy — providing cash flow while your most valuable practice asset (yourself) goes under repair — is one of the most important assets in your investment portfolio.

Dentists uniformly admit that disability insurance is an important form of protection. However, your finding the right disability policy requires your knowing what questions to ask and what features to look for.

How Much Coverage?
If you're like most dentists, this is the initial question you ask. But it is the wrong question! Instead, it should be: "How much disability coverage can I buy?" Unfortunately, a professional cannot entirely ensure his monthly income. Insurance companies permit you to buy only a limited amount of coverage approximating only 60 percent of your income.

You cannot exceed this figure by going to several different insurance companies. However, you

can obtain additional protection by adding group or
association coverage after you have purchased your
individual policies. Consequently, most dentists
should try to secure the maximum amount of individual coverage they are allowed. After their peak
earning years have passed, they can reduce their
coverage if they so desire. All of my clients recognize that their ability to generate an income is their
most valuable asset. Maintaining their families'
lifestyles and standards of living is of paramount
importance. Therefore, they always try to buy as
much individual protection as they can and add to
that protection annually. They then augment this
individual coverage with their local association coverage.

Which Is Least Expensive?

This second question also is the wrong one to ask
for disability insurance! It might be appropriate if you
were shopping for a life insurance policy that results in a one-time claim that pays the same lump
sum regardless of the premium you pay for it. However, a disability insurance policy has contractual
benefit provisions determining if, when, and how
much you will receive on a claim. Over the years
you may have one or several claims generated by
different or similar circumstances; if, when, and how
much the insurance company will pay you depends
on the company's interpretation of its contractual
provisions.

The right question in shopping for a disability
insurance policy should be: "How do I choose the
right company that will promptly pay disability benefits?" You want to buy from a financially strong company with a reputation for promptly paying claims.
To be safe, you should buy from a carrier with 10

consecutive years of A-plus rating from A.M. Best Company, which ranks insurance carriers according to their financial strength. Only a few companies write most of the high-quality individual disability policies, but not for every occupation. Some slant most of their policies to high-income executives and professionals such as yourself.

Provisions

There are several provisions to look for in a quality disability policy:

Waiting (elimination) period — This is the period between the time your disability occurs and the time your disability benefits begin. This period is usually expressed in terms of 30, 90, or 180 days—policies vary on the length of a waiting period. You do not receive any disability benefits during this time.

One way to reduce your costs of disability insurance is to select a longer elimination period. A policy with a 90-day elimination period is about 20 percent less expensive than one with a 30-day wait. A 180-day period can save you another 15 percent in premium. It is wise to buy a policy with a longer elimination period only if you know that your income will continue temporarily — either from accounts receivable, savings, investments or from a written agreement with your professional associates. Before you establish your waiting period, please remember that you will not receive your first benefit payment until approximately 30 days after the elimination period has been satisfied.

RULE: Select a longer elimination period if you can protect yourself against short-term disabilities without the need for insurance.

Length of benefits — The benefit period begins when the waiting period ends. The benefit period represents the maximum length of time during which your disability benefits are paid. Normally expressed in years, the benefit periods that a particular insurance carrier may offer can be one, five, or 10 years, or to age 65. Obviously, the premiums for longer benefit periods will be greater than those for shorter periods. Because many dentists continue to work into their later years, modern policies provide for a continuation of coverage while they are practicing full time after age 65. The benefits usually are paid for a maximum of two years, and coverage may end at age 70 or 72, depending upon the company selected.

RULE: Purchase a policy with a benefit period no less than to age 65. If you suffer a disability, it would be financially catastrophic if your disability benefits terminated prematurely because of a short benefit period. You should save premium dollars by selecting a long elimination period and should invest premium dollars by selecting a long benefit period. Unfortunately, too many ill-advised and ill-informed dentists follow a contrary philosophy. They protect themselves against temporary or short-term disabilities, which they can handle without insurance, but they leave themselves vulnerable to long-term disabilities.

Definition of disability — The "total disability" of the dentist is the event that triggers the commencement of the waiting period as well as the payment of the benefit amount. Therefore, your policy's definition of the phrase "total disability" can either be your shield or your Achilles' heel. It determines under what events and circumstances you will be paid benefits.

For example, unpleasant as the prospect may be, imagine yourself to be a peridontist who has had a heart attack, partial paralysis or stroke. The misfortune keeps you from performing the surgical skills of your profession, but when you make a partial recovery, you take a teaching position with the local university. Or, perhaps you practice general dentistry, but not your specialty. Will you still collect on your disability insurance?

Good policies would provide full disability benefits, regardless of what you earn as a professor or a general practitioner because you earn nothing in your specialty. The less desirable policies would reduce your benefits because you are still earning income in a professional capacity. The inferior policies would terminate your benefits entirely once you began earning income in your new position as a professor or general practitioner.

What definition of disability do you need in your policy? It should specify that you are totally disabled when an illness or accident prevents you from performing the "substantial and material duties of your regular occupation." This definition, which is often referred to as the "his occ" definition, is a liberal one that provides you benefits if you cannot perform in your specialty. You would collect your benefits even if you resume the practice of dentistry but in a different branch of the profession.

A second definition of total disability provides that you are totally disabled when an illness or accident prevents you from performing the important duties of your regular occupation or "any other occupation for which you are suited as a result of education, training, and experience." This definition is less desirable than the "his occ" definition, but is not unreasonably strict.

Most dentists try to return to work within their own profession after a disability. This is normal be cause they want to reestablish their earnings, be most effective, and find opportunities for part-time work, whether it be in their own or a colleague's practice. For this reason, the insurance industry has introduced a new concept that is concerned only with the degree of income loss you have suffered because of a partial disability and not with the duties you have performed to earn that income. For that reason, your "own occupation" policy should also cover a partial disability that will provide you with a partial benefits, or "residual benefits."

Without a partial disability clause, your earning a small amount within your occupation would completely terminate all benefits. For example, now consider yourself as a partially disabled dentist; you are forced to cut back on your office hours and you see your income drop from $100,000 a year to $50,000. Having residual coverage you would collect noth-ing because you are not totally disabled.

Watch out for loopholes though. Many policies pay residual benefits only if a period of total disability — sometimes as long as 12 months — has occurred first. And several policies limit how long the benefits will be paid if partial disability occurs after age 55. Many insurers will pay benefits for only 18 to 24 months. After age 55 is the very time the risk of disability to yourself is greatest. Therefore, invest in a policy that will make payments to age 65, regardless of when your disability begins.

RULE: Acquire a policy that defines you as being disabled if you are unable to perform the important duties of your regular occupation. This permits you to collect benefits even if you should pursue a different occupation to stay within your profession but engage in different activities and duties of your profession.

Partial or residual benefits to cover a partial dis-ability are a must. Residual benefits are especially important to you if you are self-employed and cannot rely on anyone to pick up the slack at your office. Because you are a conscientious dentist, you are eager to return to work, even on a part-time basis, as soon as possible after an illness or accident. The opportunity to make a slow comeback can save you from overtaxing yourself and increase your chances of a full recovery. So, you must have a policy that provides partial benefits. This will make up for your reduced income from only part-time work.

Lastly, insist on seeing a sample copy of your disability contract before you sign. How much and when you are entitled to your benefits is found in the written language of the policy and not in the verbal representations of the insurance agent.

Renewability — Two things you do not want to happen after you purchase a policy are having your premiums raised or your coverage cancelled. Some inexpensive policies permit an insurer to do either. An important part of your disability income policy is its continuance provision — the clause that spells out your rights with regard to continuation or renewability of your policy. In most disability policies purchased by individuals, the renewability provision is one of three types: (1) renewable at the company's option; (2) guaranteed renewable, and (3) noncancellable and guaranteed renewable.

- You place yourself in a vulnerable position if you purchase a policy that is renewable only at the insurer's option. As the premium due date approaches, the company has the right to inform you that the policy is going to be discontinued.
- When a policy is guaranteed renewable un-

til age 65, you have the right to continue the policy until that age; however, the insurance company retains the right to increase your premiums if it does the same for everyone in a particular "class." What constitutes a "class" differs from one carrier to another. One example is a large group of policyholders with some common characteristic such as residency in the same state. For this reason, you should exercise caution in buying guaranteed renewable disability income insurance.

- When a policy is noncancellable and guaranteed renewable to age 65, you have the right to continue the coverage to age 65. Most importantly, the company does not have the right to increase the premium above that specified in the policy, nor does the company have the right to cancel your coverage. This is the best type of policy because it both guarantees renewal and freezes the premium at its original level for as long as you keep the insurance. This type of coverage will be more expensive and more difficult to purchase.

RULE: Acquire a policy that is noncancellable and guaranteed renewable to age 65. Otherwise, you are taking unnecessary and foolish chances. In the long run, this form of protection is the cheapest of all.

Group Coverage

Various professional associations, such as the American Dental Association, offer group policies to their members. How does association disability coverage measure up to the ideal individual contract?

The initial premiums are usually less expensive than those of individual policies. But, in most cases, these premiums increase automatically the older you get. Also, the insurance carrier reserves the right to increase the premiums of all of the group members if losses approach the carrier's unprofitability zone. If you, the dentist, project yourself to age 65 and calculate the total premiums you would have paid for your group insurance (while also assuming your group carrier will never raise its premiums for your group), you will find that you would have paid about the same for the group coverage as you would have paid for individual, quality, noncancellable, and fixed-premium coverage.

No association group policy is truly noncancellable. The insurance carrier always retains the right to drop the entire group or raise premiums to an unreasonably high level. This does not happen often, but it has happened in the past. When it occurs, large groups try to find a replacement carrier; however, new rules usually apply. These rules are invariably geared to protect the new carrier that has taken over an unprofitable program. The new carrier has no intentions of permitting this unprofitability to recur. Therefore, if you stop practicing dentistry or leave the association sponsoring your plan, your policy may be cancelled individually while all the others in the group remain in force.

Treat your group disability insurance as a supplement to, not a substitute for, your own individual policy. The group disability coverage can be a useful and valuable adjunct to your and your family's security, especially when your available resources do not permit you to buy all the quality individual coverage you need and desire. But group coverage simply cannot offer the iron-clad guarantees and the options that quality individual policies can.

Planning for Disability

The most valuable asset to your dental practice and to your family is yourself, not your home, your cars, your X-ray equipment, or your operatories. Your most valuable asset is your continuing ability to generate an income.

Your willingness to plan for mishaps by insuring your home, home furnishings, car, and professional equipment from fire, theft, or other damage is proper and certainly prudent.

However, when you recognize that your chances of becoming disabled are 144 times greater than your chances of having your home burn to the ground, your priorities may change.

You are a real, not a fictional, $6 million man or woman based on 40 years of average gross annual earnings of $150,000 per year. With this sudden realization, your insuring a $6 million income-producing asset should take on greater importance than it used to. And rightfully so.

The market for disability insurance is complex. Given the wide variety of disability insurance choices, it is no surprise that so many dentists make either no decision or the easiest one possible — a small group policy.

However, you should plan for the possibility of a disability by reviewing your policies if you have the time, patience, and knowledge. If not, find an independent broker who specializes in disability insurance for dentists.

The independent broker can show you any quality company's product and help you make the right decision as to what coverage fits your lifestyle.

I will highlight here some of the critical aspects of disability insurance.

1) Protect your most valuable asset: yourself.
2) Purchase a policy with a benefit period that extends at least to age 65.
3) To save costs, select a longer elimination period if you can protect yourself without insurance for the short-term.
4) Make sure your policy covers your ability to perform your particular job at your most active level.
5) Make sure your policy is non-cancelable and guaranteed renewable to age 65. Beware of group coverage on this account. Some only offer five-year coverage.
6) Review a written statement of the provisions of your policy before you purchase it.

Finally, while increased life expectancy has driven the cost of life insurance down, it had the opposite effect on the cost of disability insurance. Don't look for a bargain at the expense of adequate coverage. And as I stated before, consider only highly rated companies for this critical protection.

Long Term Care Insurance

No one that I know likes to talk about insurance of any kind. If you plan on living a long life — you have a 48% chance of requiring some kind of long-term care in the future. Either nursing home, assisted living, or extended at-home care. In my part of the country, that would cost $2,000 to $3,000 each month. If you have $1,000,000 plus, you can pay it out of cash flow. If you are broke, the state will pick up the tab. If you are in between, please do not go without this protection. There is a 1 in 88 chance that your house would burn in your lifetime. Is it insured? You have a 1 in 70 chance of being involved in a car accident. For ages 65 and over, the chances of requiring Long-Term Care is 4 out of 10. Congratulations, you just might be the first generation to need it. That's when it is less costly.

Types to buy: The Chevrolet or the Rolls Royce. The Chevrolet is basic coverage, use it or lose it, like term life insurance. The Rolls Royce acts an investment vehicle, in other words, if you don't need coverage, they return some of your premium. Don't grow old without it!

Chapter 10

Structuring your Estate: Probates, Trusts,
and Tenancy

"Money isn't everything as long as you have enough."

Malcom Forbes

Why Plan?

You've invested a lot of time figuring out how to fund your future through effective financial planning. Have you given any thought to what happens to all of your money when time runs out? If you want to be in charge of who gets what when you no longer need or want it, you must have a plan that spells that out.

"Oh, no, another plan!" you cry. You may dread the thought, but estate planning is essential to protect the fruits of your labor for your heirs. If you don't direct the disposition of your assets, someone else will — and not necessarily to your liking or intention. This becomes especially important when you leave behind the most precious legacy — your children.

Morbid as it seems, I am sure you want your death to go as smoothly as possible for your survivors (okay, at least for some of them). To assure that the transfer of your assets happens with maximum efficiency and minimum cost, you should seek the advice of a qualified expert. I cannot stress enough the importance of enlisting an attorney who specializes in probates and trusts to take you through the necessary steps for setting up your estate. If you screw up your home improvement project, you can call a carpenter to straighten it out; you don't get a second chance if you botch the final disposition of your assets. So, don't try this at home, kids.

Who gets what, when, how, and for what reason? That is what your estate plan will direct. Whether it be guardianship of your minor children or ownership of the family treasures, it is an open question unless answered by legally executed documents. The rest of this chapter will examine possible means for achieving your final goals under the guidance of your attorney.

Estate Taxes

The high cost of dying is probably not a new concept to you. Are you aware, however, that the expenses of death may extend well beyond the colossal cost of medical care and the price of a funeral? The average cost of settling an estate in America is 7%. In addition, estate taxes, for example, may deplete your estate up to 55%! I'm not opposed to giving Uncle Sam his due, but do you really want to make him the major beneficiary of your life's work?

While you're alive, you pay taxes on your property, purchases, and income: in other words, on every conceivable object and act. In death it is more of the same. Yes, a tax ranging from 37%-55% is levied on your assets as soon as you die. There is an old saying about the inescapability of death and taxes. Now you know for sure that the Grim Reaper and Uncle Sam have been in cahoots all along.

Estate taxes are due within nine months of the time of death. A tax credit for estates up to $625,000 currently enables that amount to be transferred without federal estate tax. Through the unlimited marital deduction, spouses may currently transfer all of their assets without estate taxes.

Before you heave a sigh of relief at the generous $625,000 allowance, make sure you have included everything you own in your total asset total. All real estate, savings, securities, vehicles, investments, pensions, retirement plans, and personally owned life insurance policies must be part of this total. Are you still sliding in under the limit? The $625,000 will grow to $1,000,000 over the next decade, thank-you Washington.

Figures #43 and #44 illustrate what can happen to an estate that is transferred first to a spouse, then to other heirs when the second spouse dies in the tenth year. The

original value of the married couple's combined estate is
$1,400,000 including the life insurance value. At an 8%
annual growth rate, the value of the estate will be
$2,790,710. Administration and federal taxes total
$1,069,029 or approximately 38% of the estate. The heirs
will receive $1,721,680.

Here are five ways to handle the costs of settling and
estate.

1. **Gifting.** This involves giving gifts of up to
$10,000 per person to as many people as you
wish without taxable consequence. In this way,
you may either reduce the amount of the estate
to the tax-free limit, or at least reduce it to an
amount requiring a smaller percentage to tax.
Consult your tax counselor.

2. **Providing cash for the tax within the estate.**
You may keep enough cash in the estate to pay
the tax. Weigh this option against the potential
for return on this cash were it invested elsewhere.
Keep in mind that estate taxes are due within nine
months, in cash — not chickens.

3. **Liquidating parts of the estate.** You may not
be able to time your death with a favorable turn
of the economic cycle. This method has the inherent risk of forcing the sale of investments when
they may not be at their optimum value.

4. **The heirs borrow the money.** If your heirs are
credit-worthy, they can borrow money to pay the
estate taxes. If interest rates are high, this could
be a costly alternative.

5. **Purchasing life insurance to pay the tax at
death.** You can purchase a life insurance policy
with a death benefit equal to the estimated estate
tax. This benefit would be paid immediately following the death of the insured and would provide sufficient cash to cover the taxes. Although

current premiums are due, the benefit is funded with cents on the dollar.

Survivorship life insurance with the death benefit payable upon the second death is also available. This reduces the cost dramatically and is ideal for married people where the unlimited marital deduction will apply.

The death benefit will also be received free of income tax, and if structured properly, could also be free of federal estate tax.

Figure #45 illustrate each of the five options listed above. The enormous cost of borrowing to pay the estate costs is graphically illustrated. The most cost effective is, obviously, the purchase of the life insurance policy with the death benefit equal to the estate tax.

On the receiving end, an inheritance is more cost effective than a gift. The tax-free ceiling for gifts is $10,000. For an inheritance, it is currently $625,000. If you inherit a stock, your cost basis when you sell it, under current tax law, is the value on the date of your benefactor's death.

If it is a gift, you are given the cost base of the giver. If the stock has experienced a large increase in value over the years, a gift makes it your taxable gain.

Figure #43

The High Cost of Dying with Probate
(All-to-spouse Arrangement)

Combined Current Net Estates	$1,200,000
Estimated Growth Rate	8%
Life Insurance in the Estate	$200,000
Probate and/or Administration Costs	7%

216

Years From Now	Projected Estate Until 2nd Death*	Administration Costs at 2nd Death**	Fed. Estate Tax at Time of 2nd Death	Total Estate Costs at 2nd Death	Percentage of Estate Lost to Expenses
0	$1,400,000	$ 84,000	$283,880	$367,880	26%
1	$1,496,000	$ 90,720	$322,270	$412,990	28%
2	$1,599,680	$ 97,978	$363,766	$461,744	29%
3	$1,711,654	$105,816	$410,627	$516,443	30%
4	$1,832,587	$114,281	$461,238	$575,519	31%
5	$1,963,194	$123,424	$515,897	$639,320	33%
6	$2,104,249	$133,297	$574,928	$708,226	34%
7	$2,256,589	$143,961	$643,188	$787,149	35%
8	$2,421,116	$155,478	$718,163	$873,641	36%
9	$2,598,806	$167,916	$799,136	$967,052	37%

Years From Now	Projected Estate Until 2nd Death*	Administration Costs at 2nd Death**	Fed. Estate Tax at Time of 2nd Death	Total Estate Costs at 2nd Death	Percentage of Estate Lost to Expenses
10	$ 2,790,710	$ 181,350	$ 877,680	$1,069,030	38%
11	$ 2,997,967	$ 195,858	$ 984,055	$1,179,912	39%
12	$ 3,221,804	$ 211,526	$1,088,139	$1,299,665	40%
13	$ 3,463,549	$ 228,448	$1,200,550	$1,428,998	41%
14	$ 3,724,632	$ 246,724	$1,321,954	$1,568,678	42%
15	$ 4,006,603	$ 266,462	$1,453,070	$1,179,533	43%
20	$ 5,793,149	$ 391,520	$2,283,814	$2,675,335	46%
25	$ 8,418,170	$ 575,272	$3,504,449	$4,079,721	48%
30	$12,275,188	$ 845,263	$5,369,459	$6,214,722	51%
35	$17,942,414	$1,241,969	$8,268,244	$9,510,213	53%

Projected Estate Until 2nd Death. This column represents the growth of the total taxable estate based upon the estimate at the top of the page.

Administration Costs at Death. This column represents the probate costs of the estate unless the individual has a living trust established. Under a living trust, probate costs would be avoided.

Federal Estate Tax at Time of 2nd Death. This column represents the estate tax due upon the death of the second spouse. The unlimited marital deduction will prevent any estate taxes upon the first death.

Total Estate Costs at 2nd Death. This column represents the total of both probate costs and estate taxes. If a living trust were established, the amount in column 2 would be subtracted.

* Typically there will not be a death tax when the first spouse dies because of the Unlimited Marital Deduction. Life insurance proceeds are included in the estate, but the face amount does not increase along with the other assets.

** Life insurance proceeds are not included here in determining the probate expenses.

*** Under current tax law, subject to change. Consult your tax advisor.

Figure #43

High Cost of Dying with Probate -- Assumes 2nd
Death in 10 Years
(All-to-spouse Arrangement)

Projected Estate Size: $2,790,709
LESS Administration Costs: $ 181,349
LESS Federal Estate Taxes: $ 887,680
Net to Heirs: $1,721,680

Administration Costs

Federal
Estate Tax   Assets to Heirs

Assets to Heirs. This represents the net amount of the
estate which will pass to the heirs after probate and estate
taxes.
Administration Costs. This represents the amount of the
estate lost to probate costs.
Federal Estate Tax. This represents the amount of the
estate lost to the estate tax.

Figure #44

Ways to Pay Estate Costs

ESTATE SETTLEMENT COSTS:	$ 978,354
Cash in the Estate:	$ 978,354
Sale of Stocks and Bonds:	$1,017,488
Liquidate at 40% Discount Rate:	$1,630,590
Borrow Cash at 10% for 30 Years:	$3,113,492
LIFE INSURANCE	$ 66,000

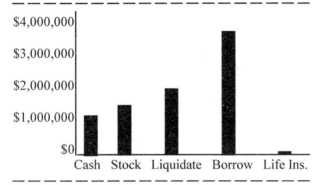

Cash. This represents the total dollar cost of paying the estate tax in cash.

Stock. This represents the total dollar cost of paying the tax by liquidating available stocks.

Liquidate. This represents the total dollar cost of liquidating other investments such as real estate or personal assets to pay the tax, based upon the sale of assets at 60% of value.

Borrow. This represents the total dollar cost of paying the tax by having the heirs borrow the cash equal to the estate tax at an interest rate of 9% for 30 years.

Life Insurance. This represents the total dollar cost of purchasing a universal life insurance policy with a death benefit equal to the estate tax due.

Probate

Probate is the legal process of distributing your assets to your beneficiaries upon your death. This can be a fairly straightforward process if your estate is in order and you have a proper will. The national average for the cost of the probate is approximately 7%. Average, though, can be a tricky word. In most cases, cost is less than 7%.

A will makes public the manner in which you want your estate to be distributed. In most cases, it must be a written document to be accepted as the plan you desired. I am sure you are a better judge than the state of who is an appropriate guardian for your children. I am also certain that you have your own opinion on who should take over ownership of your worldly goods.

The entire probate process is a public one. Upon your death, your personal effects not only cease to be yours, but they cease to be personal. You may find it an interesting adventure to examine the court documents on the settlement of a very large estate if you have time on your hands to browse and snoop. The entire inventory of the deceased's worldly goods is available for examination.

In addition to the curiosity factor, there is an educational benefit to examining the record of the probate process. This activity can help you gain some familiarity with the step-by-step legal process of probate from filing of the death certificate to the final distribution of goods.

If you don't have a will, take care of it quickly. Otherwise, you might die intestate. Sounds bad, doesn't it? It's not a dirty word actually, but it can prove to be a nasty state of affairs for your heirs. Intestate means that you have no written will or estate plan. It also means the state will decide what happens to your assets and who oversees the process. Typically, this can mean your spouse may receive only half — possibly less — of your estate, and the rest will be divided equally among your surviving children or grandchildren. It may also mean that probate will erode an even larger portion of your estate.

Your will should be updated every five to six years or sooner in the event that you experience a major change in your circumstances. Marriage, divorce, or the birth or independence of a child may impact your point of view regarding distribution of your assets.

Let me reiterate the advice I gave earlier: Have a qualified specialist handle this part of your estate plan for you. Since your will must pass through the judicial system, it should be guided by one who is well-versed in that system.

Trusts

"To trust or not to trust?" That is a question many people forget to ask when structuring their estates. In my opinion, trusts are too aggressively marketed. This results in people who may not really need them using them. So before you agonize over what kind of trust to use, step back and ask yourself if you need to use one at all. Remember: You don't need to a chainsaw to cut a cheesecake.

You can set up a trust either through your will or as a living trust. A trust you designate in your will is irrevocable, unable to be altered. You can set up either revocable or irrevocable trusts throughout the course of your life. A trust allows you to very specifically control what actions may be taken with the money you put into the trust.

Do you need to set up a trust? You need to examine your personal circumstances before you answer that question. For example, I am fairly confident that, should anything happen to his mother and me, that my teenage son will act responsibly and rationally with the assets he inherits. I believe that he will keep the money in the hands of a good investment counselor, go on to college and build the career he dreams of — just as we have always planned it. Ha, ha.

Your kids may lean towards a fast, red car and a short-lived affluence instead of pursuing the goals you set together. You know them best. Let reality be your guiding principle.

Here is a brief overview of types of trusts designed to suit a variety of purposes. DO NOT accept this as gospel. ONLY a qualified lawyer should dispense legal counsel that you can count on.

Revocable Living Trusts

This is a trust in which you place some or all of your assets while you are alive. The terms of this trust can be changed or revoked by you at any time. You can withdraw or add assets for any reason you choose. Because you have complete control over the trust and its assets, you are viewed as the owner for federal income tax and estate tax purposes.

While you maintain control, you also achieve important benefits. The trust provides uninterrupted professional financial management of trust assets for you and avoids expensive, cumbersome guardianship proceedings if you are ill or incapacitated. A properly drawn revocable trust may also help you avoid unnecessary estate or inheritance taxes and generation-skipping taxes.

Additionally, the assets in a revocable trust do not go through the delay, expense, red tape, and publicity of probate. A revocable trust provides for confidentiality and privacy. No one but the beneficiaries need to know the terms of the trust, its assets or beneficiaries. Trust resources are generally available to your family immediately after death.

These trusts can also be designed to address your specific family problems such as minor children, and handicapped or spendthrift family members. Your spouse and children can be protected from unscrupulous persons by having the trust continue after your death until they are ready to manage on their own.

Irrevocable Living Trust

Once you place assets into this type of trust, the terms of the trust cannot be altered and you cannot get the property back from the trust. The trusts are generally used to save federal and state income taxes and inheritance taxes.

Life Insurance Trust

This type of irrevocable trust receives the proceeds of a life insurance policy in order to keep them out of your taxable estate. It can be important in providing immediate liquidity to your estate for taxes or your beneficiaries to avoid stress sales of closely held business or real estate. It can also provide significant long-term estate tax and generation-skipping tax savings for your children and grandchildren.

Minor's and Education Trusts

These trusts are used to convey gifts of assets to children or grandchildren. You may give a minor child up to $10,000 a year, ($20,000 if you are married), in trust, without filing a federal tax return or paying any gift taxes, under current tax law. Since the trust and/or the minor are generally in lower income tax brackets, income tax savings enhance savings for such purposes as education. Additionally, such trusts provide more flexibility, tax benefits, and control of assets than do gifts to a uniform gift minor's account. Assets in such trusts also avoid taxation in your estate. Consult your tax advisor about the recently imposed "kiddie-tax".

Charitable Remainder Trusts

These tax-advantaged trusts allow you to provide for income for yourself or someone else from assets that you designate for charity. You get an immediate income tax deduction for a gift to the trust, and you and/or others you designate receive income for life from the trust. Ultimately the property goes to the charity. You can also avoid capital gains taxes and increase your income if appreciated, low-yielding property is used to fund the trust. The trusts assets are insulated from attack by creditors, and in most cases avoid federal and state death taxes and probate.

Credit Shelter Trusts

If you are married and have assets of $625,000 or more, this trust plan can insure that you and your spouse maximize the use of federal estate tax exemptions available to both of you. Upon the death of the first spouse, $625,000 is set aside in such a trust with the balance of the estate given to the surviving spouse outright or in trust. Assets in this trust provide benefits for the survivor but avoid estate taxes on the survivor's death. For example, on the estate of $1,200,000, this plan can avoid any unnecessary estate taxes of approximately $235,000, under current tax laws, which of course are subject to change.

Charitable Lead Trust

The trust pays income to charities for a term of years,

after which the principal is paid to you or your designated beneficiaries. Although it can provide income tax benefits, its primary use is to substantially discount federal estate taxes and generation-skipping taxes.

Grantor Retained Income Trust (GRIT)

You can transfer cash or income producing property to a trust, retaining the income for a term of years after which the assets belong to your heirs. The benefit of this plan is that you substantially reduce estate taxes on the trust assets and appreciation of such assets if you survive the term of the trust.

Once again, let a qualified professional be your guiding hand. Like extraction of your wisdom teeth or heart by-pass surgery, this is not a do-it-yourself project. As in the case of any other professional service, the level and cost of this service should be discussed up front and agreed upon.

Tenancy: The Wisdom of Togetherness in Ownership

Joint tenancy is a great idea from young couples. In my opinion, benefits decline as age increases.

I will spend the rest of this section outlining the disadvantages of joint tenancy which I feel outweigh the advantages. However, if you have already put some assets in joint tenancy, don't rush right out and switch them back. You may trigger a new problem. A certified accountant can help you undo what you have unwittingly done.

Let's look at a painfully common argument against joint tenancy in advancing years. It seemed like a good idea for Mom and Dad to have their property jointly held. That way, no matter who passed away first, the other would simply remove the name of the deceased from the title and own the property outright. But with 50% ownership, comes 100% use.

What if, however, Dad gets Alzheimer's disease or dementia and needs to go in a nursing home. Now Mom is alone in the house they own together. Maybe the house becomes too much for her to handle alone; maybe now she needs to sell it to help pay for Dad's care.

It may be painful enough for her to have to sell their home; it may be even more painful when Mom discovers she cannot sell it without Dad's signature. She now has to go to court and have him judged incapable of making decisions before she can exercise control over the property.

It may be just her luck that on the day the court appointed authority visits Dad in the nursing home, he has a rare moment of lucidity. "What do you mean she wants to sell the house?" he thunders. "I'm gonna be fine in a couple more weeks; then I'll be back home." The house gets frozen and cannot be sold.

In this situation, Mom and Dad are pitted against each other in the eyes of the court. Doesn't that just make Mom's day?

The preceding was an actual case near my hometown and, sadly, not a rarity.

Sometimes there are temptations to put children's names on some of our assets with rights of survivorship. Don't. In the strictest sense of the law, this is considered a gift. If the value is over $10,000, it is taxable. That's not all. If you are audited, the IRS can decide that the one in the highest marginal tax bracket is the one liable for the tax — not Mom who is retired. It's the old 50% ownership, 100% use snag again.

Do not put assets in other people's names unless you truly intend them to receive those assets. If an individual asset is over $10,000, don't do it at all, until you get guidance on the potential taxation.

Prudent planning enabled you to make money. The same kind of planning will enable your estate to save money. To preserve the value and control the disposition of your legacy, seek the help of a qualified professional in building the appropriate plan.

Chapter 11

Building and Monitoring Your Plan

"Investors don't plan to fail; most just fail to plan."

Source Unknown

Bradley Gummow

In the preceding ten chapters, I provided you with resources that would enable you to take stock of your personal financial picture and enhance your understanding of the arena in which the financial game is played. I certainly hope that I made an indisputable case for the necessity of having a deliberate financial plan.

In the course of digesting the text and completing the worksheets, you may have either fine-tuned existing skills or developed new ones that will enable you to participate productively in the money game.

In the first chapter, you stated and quantified the goals for your short- and long-range financial future and took inventory of your investments. Chapter 2 introduced you to the Nobel prize-winning Modern Portfolio Theory which proposes that proper diversification and balance of investments are the keys to a successful financial portfolio. You were called upon to analyze whether your existing allocation of assets was in harmony with the goals you set. Subsequent chapters provided overviews of the variety of available investment vehicles with editorial comment on their individual risks and rewards and their collective roles in relation to an integrated balance of investments.

I am going to start this chapter on building your plan by telling you what you will *not* find here. You will not be instructed to invest a particular percentage of your income. You will not find a list of particular CD's, stocks, or bonds to purchase. Nor will you be told a particular dollar amount to channel into each investment category. You will not be told if or when to liquidate any of your assets in favor of others. In fact, I will not tell you to do anything.

At this point, you may be wondering, "Why am I reading this chapter at all?" Actually, you will be more of a writer than a reader in Chapter 11. It is time to build your plan. You have set your goals and assembled your resources; you are in the driver's seat.

Do you get the impression that I am avoiding taking responsibility for your investment decisions? Good! That's exactly the impression I am trying to give. I have not seen the first figure of your financial profile. Would your doctor diagnose you by telepathy?

At this point, you have assembled all financial data pertinent to your specific case and have had a chance to analyze it in a new light. You are the one in control of and accountable for what happens to your money. You are the one who will experience the consequences of those decisions; you must, therefore, make them.

My purpose in this chapter is to provide you with two-fold support as you tackle the task at hand. First, I will review with you the factors in the economic environment that have critical impact on the performance of your invested dollars. Secondly, I will provide a sample matrix for each of three investment stages in your life accompanied by a worksheet for comparing the appropriate sample to your current situation.

An integrated diversity of investments is the most likely to achieve your financial goals. Modern Portfolio Theory extols the merits of diversifying by category: debt (bonds, CD's, annuities, etc.), equities (stocks, real estate, etc.), and cash/cash equivalents (savings, checking, short-term CD's, treasury bills). It is also beneficial to diversify by due date — to balance (ladder) the maturity dates of your various investments. Pay attention to duration. Make sure you can afford to leave long-term money invested for enough time to reap full advantage of the economic cycle. You will not have easy access to money invested in debts or equities, so keep this in mind when you anticipate what cash you will need to cover living expenses or emergencies.

Consider the dependability of a potential investment. Review the discussion of risk and reward and find your comfort zone. Review also the investment mistakes to avoid. Investment is a systematic, not a mystical, process.

Beware of factors that devalue your purchasing power. Inflation and the taxman are the duo that dips into the till the deepest. Prudent decisions take them into account.

Worksheet #6 will allow you to compare your current allocation of assets to the recommended one for your particular financial stage. Using your completed Asset Allocation Survey as a resource, fill in the appropriate information on the Asset Allocation Format Worksheet.

Figure #46 provides sample matrices for both moderately conservative and aggressive investors in three age groups. Find your style and stage. Now fill in the recommended allocation on your Asset Allocation Worksheet.

ASSET ALLOCATION FORMAT SHEET

	Current Asset Allocation	*Recommended Asset Allocation
Cash/Cash Equivalents	$ %	$ %
Fixed Income	$ %	$ %
Stocks	$ %	$ %
Property Ownership	$ %	$ %
Tangible Assets	$ %	$ %
Totals:	$	$

Figure #46

Asset Allocation Matrix

Age 20-39	Moderately Conservative	Agressive
Cash/Cash Equivalents	20%	20%
Fixed Income	20%	10%
Stocks	35%	40%
Property Ownership	20%	25%
Tangible Assets	5%	5%
Age 40-59		
Cash/Cash Equivalents	10%	10%
Fixed Income	50%	35%
Stocks	25%	35%
Property Ownership	10%	15%
Tangible Assets	5%	5%
Age 60+		
Cash/Cash Equivalents	5%	5%
Fixed Income	65%	50%
Stocks	25%	30%
Property Ownership	10%	10%
Tangible Assets	5%	5%

Rules of Thumb:

Cash/Cash Equivalents: If you are employed, use 2 to 3 months of expenses to determine the % of this category. If you have over $500,000 in income generating assets, lesser % can be allocated to this category. If you have excessive income over expenses, lesser % can be allocated to this category.

Property Ownership and/or Tangible Assets: If you do not need dollars allocated to these categories, you may wish to allocate the same monies to the stocks category.

INVESTMENT SUITABILITY

Cash/Cash Equivalents $ _____

*Suit-ability	Assets	Amount	Income or %	Taxable or Non-
	Savings Accounts			
	Checking Accounts			
	T-Bills			
	Certificates of Deposit			
	Tax-Free Money Markets			
	Money Markets			

* S=Suitability page only, R=Recommended page only, B=Both.

Winning The Money Game Made Easy

Fixed Income $_____

*Suit-ability	Assets	Amount	Income or %	Taxable or Non-
	Real Estate Investment Trusts			
	Convertible Bonds			
	Fixed Annuities			
	Int'l Bonds			
	Trust Deeds			
	Govt. Securties			
	Zero-Coupon Bonds			
	Municipal Bonds			
	Corporate Bonds			
	Managed Bond Funds			

Bradley Gummow

Stocks $ _____

*Suitability	Assets	Amount	Income
	Int'l Stocks		
	Variable Annuities		
	Utility Stocks		
	Growth Stocks		
	Blue-Chip Stocks		
	Managed Equity Funds		

Property Ownership $ _____

*Suitability	Assets	Amount	Income
	Natural Resource LP		
	Land		
	Cable TV LP		
	Real Estate LP		
	Equipment Leasing LP		
	Tax Credit LP		
	Gas & Oil LP		
	Commerical Real Estate		
	Residential Real Estate		

Bradley Gummow

Tangible Assets $_____

*Suitability	Assets	Amount	Income
	Natural Resource Funds		
	Gold Mutual Funds		
	Gold/Silver Coins		

* S=Suitability page only, R=Recommended page only, B=Both.

PORTFOLIO REVIEW SCHEDULE

_____

_____

_____

_____

FUTURE VALUE AND INCOME ANALYSIS

Investments	***Rates of Return	Amount	Years		

Investments	***Rates of Return	Amount	Years		
Annual Contribution					
Annual Contribution					
Annual Contribution					
Annual Contribution					
TOTAL:					
ANNUAL INCOME:					
DISCOUNTED FV:					
DISCOUNTED INCOME:					

* Income stream assumes _____% annual distribution.
** Discounted future value and income assume _____% inflation.
*** Rates of return are based on past performance and reflect no indication or guarantee of future performance.

How do the two columns compare? If you have an unproductive hodge-podge, it's time to go to work. It is time to write a plan to balance and integrate your investments for maximum return.

Good luck!

Are you panicking? Then stop. At any stage you are uncomfortable making a decision on your own, it is not a crime or a shame to consult an appropriate professional whom you have provided with your complete, unexpurgated financial picture. Chapter 12 will discuss how to choose one worthy of your confidence.

Even when you have written your plan, your task is not finished. First, you will need to implement it. Then you must monitor it regularly; I suggest at least quarterly. Your task will, in fact, never be finished. This last step is an ongoing process. To survive and prosper, your plan must be a living, breathing thing that grows and makes adjustments within its environment and with your changing situation.

A responsible broker will prepare your plan *before* he/she suggests or recommends investments.

Chapter 12

Selecting a Professional -- If You Don't Go It Alone

"There is no honor in losing your money all by yourself."

Bradley L. Gummow

Once you have forged your Personal Investment plan you may — and justifiably so — experience the thrill of victory that usually follows a remarkable accomplishment. And it is a remarkable accomplishment! You have mapped out the route to your financial future, and you now know how to read the signs along the way.

You have finished perhaps the most tedious work, but the most important work — that of regular and systematic monitoring of the plan — lies ahead of you. If your plan is to be successful, it must flow and grow in harmony with a changing economic environment. It is time, therefore, to ask yourself the question, "Do I have the time, discipline, and disposition to manage this plan effectively?" Be painfully honest in your answer, or the consequences may be painful in the long run.

If you feel confident at this point to handle your personal investment plan, go forth, and may your money multiply! If your answer is, "Not really," you are not alone and should not let it damage your self worth. (It is more prudent to make sure false pride doesn't damage your financial worth.) In this case, selecting a broker or investment counselor/advisor is critical to your investment success. What you have learned here will equip you to enlist the services of someone who is qualified to help.

Many professionals stand ready and able to assist you in the planning and investment process. Among them are stockbrokers, insurance salesmen, bankers, accountants, lawyers, financial planners, investment planners, investment counselors, and investment advisors. While they may not be able to boast the sound fiscal record of Peter Lynch's seventh-grade friends, they have qualifications you may examine and evaluate to determine if they suit your style and needs.

Some are paid by hourly retainers, others on a commission basis. An advisor may be self-employed or be a member of a firm, company, or agency.

244

In any case, the primary mission of an advisor is to generate fees, or make a sale. While you are not necessarily looking for someone who worships money as a false idol, there is nothing unholy about an advisor with a healthy respect for profit. (Profit is, after all, exactly what you seek.) A true professional — the one you want on your team — will consider your needs and desires as the best means to achieving his mission.

Your search should begin by setting up meetings with two or three potential advisors. You may find them through advertising or through recommendation of friends or associates. When you go for your first interview with each one, leave your checkbook at home, and make it perfectly clear that you are there only to consider the possibility of working with them, not to start planning and investing. The meter should not be running during this first visit.

You should not make any decisions during the visit. A true professional who is looking out for your best interest does not expect you to jump in blindly. Beware of someone who pressures you to retain him on the spot or offers you a deal you must act on immediately. An advisor who tries to sell you something on the first visit is akin to a doctor who commences surgery before an exam. Both a good advisor and a good deal will remain so while you reflect over the merits on a conscientious deliberate manner. Take all the time you need; your financial future is at stake.

Remember that you are there to get a "financial physical." The diagnosis must be based on a comprehensive view. You should bring with you all pertinent financial papers, like the ones you assembled to work on your plan. Your completed worksheets will be a great help, too.

Your potential advisor should be interested in the following:

1. *Reviewing your complete tax return for at least one year.*
2. *Discussing your investment style and temperament, i.e. risk and reward expectations.*
3. *Discussing your financial goals and aspirations.*
4. *Reviewing your current investments.*
5. *Discussing your past investment successes and, as importantly, your failures.*
6. *Discussing income levels, potential liabilities, and projected long-range and ongoing expenses, i.e. education and retirement funding.*
7. *Discussing your career(s) along with your current and previous retirement plans.*

Your interest in the potential advisor should be as incisive as his is in you. Now it is your turn to ask the questions; here are some that will reveal whether the two of you will be a good match.

1. **How many accounts (clients) does the broker/advisor currently service?** I would not want to be the first, neither would I want to be number 8007. Look for someone with enough accounts to indicate experience, but not so many that he will be too busy to give you the time and consideration that you and your investment money deserve. My suggestion is to look for a range of 500 - 1500 accounts.
2. **What size accounts does the broker/advisor accept?** If he deals exclusively with skinny rabbits, how can they properly manage your elephant-sized account or vice versa? Brokers/advisors often specialize in a particular account size (within a range). It is only natural for them to

246

contact larger accounts first. Where would you fit in?

3. **What is the background or previous experience of account personnel?** I have sincere respect for all legal and ethical vocations. One does not, however, easily switch from a cab-driving career to investment advising without some dramatic education, retraining, and experience.

4. **How many years has the broker/advisor been in business?** I hate to pick on the young whippersnappers; nevertheless, a little gray hair is a wonderful teacher. Most baby boomers have grown up knowing nothing but inflation. If we are now in a period of disinflation, how will your investment behave? Experience is an excellent resource in finding the answer. Unless a broker was in business prior to 1982, he has only a textbook idea of how a true, extended bear market behaves. Call me old-fashioned, but I prefer the one who has fought both the hard and the easy battles, rather than the one who has watched them. Like anything else, there are exceptions, but for my money, I'll stick with the odds.

5. **Does the potential advisor have an area of specialty?** You are by now aware of the variety of investment opportunities available. You also know you should not do anything you don't want to do with your money. Make sure you are comfortable making the type of investments that your potential advisor predominantly makes.

6. **Does the broker/advisor employ appropriate support personnel?** Who minds the store when the advisor is out? You can feel more confident if a registered (licensed) assistant is on staff.

7. **What are the broker/advisor's strengths and weaknesses?** Human beings have both, and hon-

est one's are not reluctant to share them with you.

8. **Has the broker/dealer company ever been disciplined for any violations?** If so, what were the circumstances?

Ask the advisor for a resume or biography. Most professionals have them readily available in anticipation of client inquiry.

After interviewing the individual advisor, ask to speak to the branch manager to verify all of the information you were given. One of my most astute competitors in the business has a great saying: *"Invest your time before you invest your money."*

As I mentioned in Chapter 4, the Securities and Exchange Commission is the primary watchdog agency responsible for administering federal securities laws. In addition, the New York Stock Exchange (NYSE), American Stock Exchange (ASE), the National Association of Securities Dealers (NASD), and individual states have securities commissions that police the industry.

The NYSE, ASE, and NASD are member-owned and are highly self-regulated. Potential NYSE member firm brokers are scrutinized intensively before they are hired, and they must pass a rigorous exam before they start work.

I suggest that a financial advisor who will effectively fill your needs should possess the following characteristics:

- Is a Registered Investment Advisor.
- Is a broker for a NYSE member firm, preferably for a firm that does not sell proprietary products (this keeps your investment options open).
- Has an adequate support staff available, including a registered assistant.
- Is open and honest with information about the company and its transactions.
- Has a manageable account load consisting of

those similar to yours in style and size.

- Makes every effort to make you feel comfortable and valued.

- Has a bit of hard-earned gray hair, usually by virtue of longevity — at least thirty-five years old, or so (okay, so I'm prejudiced, but please, no hate mail from mavericks). I want him/her to know what a BEAR market is like.

Make your decision on who will manage your personal investment plan very carefully. There is no shame in seeking appropriate, professional financial help when you need it. Conversely, there is no honor in losing your money all by yourself.

Glossary

A

A.M. Best & Company. A highly regarded insurance company rating agency. Top rating assigned by A. M. Best & Company is A+ (excellent).

annuitant. Legal designation for a person who receives benefits from an annuity.

authorized stock. The maximum number of shares a corporation may issue, either common or preferred, for current and future distribution. The number is stated in the corporation's charter.

B

beneficiary. The receiver of estate proceeds or insurance policy proceeds.

blue-chip stock. Term from the high value blue chip in poker. Refers to stocks of companies that are leaders in their industry, have a proven record of profits, and history of dividend payment. Blue-chip stocks are represented in the Dow Jones 30 industrial stocks and Standard & Poor's 500 Index.

bond. A security representing debt with a maturity of ten years or more. A shorter duration is known as a "note". A bond is issued for a specific period of time and a specific interest rate.

bond ratings. A measure of credit worthiness assigned by a rating agency; i.e. Standard & Poor's, Moody's, or

Duffy & Phelps.

book value. Generally considered to be the liquidation value of a company. All assets minus intangible assets minus all liabilities.

Brady bonds. Named after Nicholas Brady, former Treasury Secretary. The Brady Plan collateralized certain foreign nation's debts with U.S. Treasury securities. Participating countries included: Mexico, Venezuela, Philippines, Costa Rica, Argentina, and others.

break-out. A technical analysis term describing a price up (advance) from a base building period.

Bundes Bank. The central reserve of Germany. It sets and maintains monetary policy for Germany. Generally regarded as the major influence on interest rates in all of Europe. The "banker's bank" of Germany.

C

capital gains. The profit (gain) of an asset sale.

collateralized mortgage obligations (CMO). A debt security secured by pools of mortgages guaranteed by government agencies or private insurers. Generally CMO's receive an AAA rating from rating agencies.

common stock. Class of ownership (equity) of a corporation. Claims of common stockholders are settled after bondholders, creditors, and preferred stockholders. Generally, common stockholders have voting rights for control of management and company policy.

compounding. Interest earning interest or dividends earning dividends. Generally increases yield/return on an investment dramatically over a long period of time.

convertibles. A bond that can be converted into shares of the common stock. Typically pay interest every six months.

corporate bond. Bonds issued by corporations to fund acquisitions or capital spending requirements. *See also* **bond**.

D

disinflation. The state of the economy when inflation has stalled. When the cost of goods and services stop climbing at inflated rates.

dividend. The portion of a company's earnings paid out to shareholders, normally on a quarterly basis.

dollar cost averaging. Purchasing the same dollar amount of a commodity, over a sustained period of time. Generally accepted as a conservative method of investing in stocks or mutual funds.

F

Farmer's Home Administration (FHA). An agency of

the U.S. Department of Agriculture. Grants loans at reasonable rates, and credit advice for families, farms, homes, and community facilities in rural areas of the United States.

Federal Home Loan Mortgage Corporation (FHLMC or Freddie Mac). Government sponsored corporation owned by FHLMC. Purchase conventional residential mortgages from FHLMC members, then repackage and resell to the public.

Federal National Mortgage Association (FNMA or Fannie Mae). Government sponsored, publicly owned corporation that serves as a secondary market for FHA insured and some conventional mortagages.

Federal Reserve Board. Statutory board responsible for setting reserve requirements, open market activities, establishing the discount rate and controlling credit in the margin purchase of securities. The board is comprised of seven members appointed by the President with the advice and consent of the Senate, for terms of 14 years. The board regulates banking and credit activity under the Federal Reserve Act of 1913.

fixed income securities. A security in which the issuer pays the owner a specific interest rate annually; i.e. notes, bonds, debentures, bills.

fundamental analysis. A method of stock selection using the underlying value of a company as its primary consideration.

G

gift tax. Tax the Federal Government levies on gifting transactions. Currently comes into effect on gifts of $10,000 (value) or more. Consult a reputable tax advisor for transactions on gifting.

Government National Mortgage Association (GNMA or Ginnie Mae). Government-owned corporation within the Department of Housing and Urban Development (HUD). Facilitates financing in the primary market by purchasing mortgages from private lenders. Sell debt securities on the secondary market guaranteeing timely payment or principal and interest.

growth stock. Equity security that is expected to increase in market value at a relatively rapid rate.

I

illiquid. Not readily available for redemption or sale. Only long-term investment money is placed in illiquid investments. Real estate is an example of a good, but illiquid investment.

income fund. Generally a mutual fund with a primary emphasis on distributing and/or reinvesting income on a monthly or quarterly basis.

inflation. An economic condition that is characterized by increases in the amount of money in circulation and rising prices of goods and services. The purchasing power of individual dollars erodes as a result.

invest. The act of placing money in an asset designed to return a larger amount upon sale of said asset.

issued stock. Refers to the number of shares of a stock that have been sold, or are outstanding.

J

junk bond. High yielding bonds with a debt rating less than investment grade; i.e. Standard & Poor's rating of BB, B, CCC, CC, C, etc. Used extensively to finance leveraged buyouts in the 1970's and 1980's. *See also* **bond**.

K

kiddie-tax. Jocular term used in describing a feature of the Tax Reform Act of 1986. Affects the taxation of children under the age of fourteen.

L

large captialization. Term used to refer to companies whose market value is over $1 billion. The formula used is the number of outstanding shares multiplied by the stock's price.

Lombard Rate. The German banking system's equivalent of the Federal Reserve's discount rate. Rate of interest charged to member banks.

long-term. An arbitrary term, generally regarded as one, two, three, or more years.

long-term capital gain. Represents profits on sales of assets that have been held one year or more. Subject to taxation. Gains are taxable; losses are deductible in most cases. *See also* **capital gains.**

M

marginal tax bracket. Marginal tax bracket is generally referred to as the highest marginal bracket that your investments are subject to.

matrix. For the purpose of this book, a matrix is the breakdown of investment categories in your portfolio; i.e. 20% cash, 30% bonds, 30% stocks, 10% real estate, 10% tangible assets.

medium capitalization. Term used to refer to companies whose market value is between $500 million and $1 billion. The formula used is the number of outstanding shares multiplied by the stock's price.

municipal bond. Bond issued by states, countries, or any taxing district. Income received is generally free of federal income tax. *See also* **bond.**